WITHD[R] D0130082

COLLEGE LIBRARY

Psyc...analysis and Storytelling

**Please return this book by the date stamped below
- if recalled, the loan is reduced to 10 days**

1 9 APR 2002 CANCELLED	1 0 NOV 2004	**RETURNED** 2 3 APR 2008
- 3 DEC 2002	**RETURNED** 1 8 JAN 2008	
2 0 DEC 2002 CANCELLED	**RETURNED** 2 3 JAN 2008	
1 3 JUN 2003		
- 7 NOV 2003		
28 / 11 / 03		
2 - CANCELLED		

Fines are payable for late return

College of Ripon & York St. John

3 8025 00338597 1

THE BUCKNELL LECTURES IN LITERARY THEORY
General Editors: Michael Payne and Harold Schweizer

The lectures in this series explore some of the fundamental changes in literary studies that have occurred during the past thirty years in response to new work in feminism, Marxism, psychoanalysis, and deconstruction. They assess the impact of these changes and examine specific texts in the light of this new work. Each volume in the series includes a critical assessment of the lecturer's own publications, an interview, and a comprehensive bibliography.

Forthcoming volumes by Barbara Johnson and Stanley Cavell.

Psychoanalysis and Storytelling

Peter Brooks

LIBRARY, UNIVERSITY COLLEGE
OF RIPON & YORK ST. JOHN
RIPON HG4 2QX

BLACKWELL
Oxford UK & Cambridge USA

Copyright © Peter Brooks 1994

Introductory and editorial matter © John S. Rickard and Harold Schweizer 1994

The right of Peter Brooks to be identified as author of this work has been asserted in accordance with the Copyright, Designs and Patents Act 1988.

First published 1994
Reprinted 1994

Blackwell Publishers, the publishing imprint of
Basil Blackwell Inc.
238 Main Street
Cambridge, Massachusetts 02142, USA

Basil Blackwell Ltd
108 Cowley Road
Oxford OX4 1JF
UK

All rights reserved. Except for the quotation of short passages for the purposes of criticism and review, no part of this publication may be reproduced, stored in a retrieval system, or transmitted, in any form or by any means, electronic, mechanical, photocopying, recording or otherwise, without the prior permission of the publisher.

Except in the United States of America, this book is sold subject to the condition that it shall not, by way of trade or otherwise, be lent, re-sold, hired out, or otherwise circulated without the publisher's prior consent in any form of binding or cover other than that in which it is published and without a similar condition including this condition being imposed on the subsequent purchaser.

Library of Congress Cataloging-in-Publication Data

Brooks, Peter, 1938–
    Psychoanalysis and Storytelling / Peter Brooks.
        p. cm.—(The Bucknell lectures in literary theory; 10)
    Includes bibliographical references and index.
    ISBN 0–631–19007–4.—ISBN 0–631–19008–2 (pbk.)
    1. Psychoanalysis and literature.   2. Criticism.   I. Title.
II. Series.
PN56. P92B76 1994
801'92—dc20   93–29667
                                                                             CIP

British Library Cataloguing in Publication Data

A CIP catalogue record for this book is available from the British Library.

Typeset in 11 on 13 pt Plantin by Pure Tech Corporation, Pondicherry, India
Printed and bound in Great Britain by Hartnolls Ltd, Bodmin, Cornwall

This book is printed on acid-free paper

Contents

Preface

Fundamental and far-reaching changes in literary studies, often compared to paradigmatic shifts in the sciences, have been taking place during the last thirty years. These changes have included enlarging the literary canon not only to include novels, poems, and plays by writers whose race, gender, or nationality had marginalized their work but also to include texts by philosophers, psychoanalysts, historians, anthropologists, social and religious thinkers, who previously were studied by critics merely as "background." The stance of the critic and student of literature is also now more in question than ever before. In 1951 it was possible for Cleanth Brooks to declare with confidence that the critic's job was to describe and evaluate literary objects, implying the relevance for criticism of the model of scientific objectivity while leaving unasked questions concerning significant issues in scientific theory, such as complementarity, indeterminacy, and the use of metaphor. Now the possibility of value-free skepticism is itself in doubt as many feminist, Marxist, and psychoanalytic theorists have stressed the inescapability of ideology and the consequent obligation of teachers and students of literature to declare their political, axiological, and aesthetic positions in order to make those positions conscious and available for examination. Such expansion and deepening of literary studies has, for many critics, revitalized their field.

Those for whom the theoretical revolution has been regenerative would readily echo, and apply to criticism, Lacan's call to revitalize psychoanalysis: "I consider it to be an urgent task to disengage from concepts that are being deadened by routine use the meaning that they regain both from a re-examination of their history and from a reflexion on their subjective foundations. That, no doubt, is the teacher's prime function."

Many practising writers and teachers of literature, however, see recent developments in literary theory as dangerous and anti-humanistic. They would insist that displacement of the centrality of the word, claims for the "death of the author," emphasis upon gaps and incapacities in language, and indiscriminate opening of the canon threaten to marginalize literature itself. In this view the advance of theory is possible only because of literature's retreat in the face of aggressive moves by new historicism, feminism, deconstruction, and psychoanalysis. Furthermore, at a time of militant conservativism and the dominance of corporate values in America and Europe, literary theory threatens to diminish further the declining audience for literature and criticism. Theoretical books are difficult to read; they usually assume that their readers possess knowledge that few have who have received a traditional literary education; they often require massive reassessments of language, meaning, and the world; they seem to draw their life from suspect branches of other disciplines: professional philosophers usually avoid Derrida; psychoanalysts dismiss Freud as unscientific; Lacan was excommunicated even by the International Psycho-Analytical Association.

The volumes in this series record part of the attempt at Bucknell University to sustain conversation about changes in literary studies, the impact of those changes on literary art, and the significance of literary theory for the humanities and human sciences. A generous grant from the Andrew W. Mellon Foundation has made possible a five-year series of visiting lectureships by internationally known participants in the reshaping of literary studies. Each volume includes a comprehensive introduction to the published work of the lecturer, the Bucknell Lectures, an interview, and a comprehensive bibliography.

Acknowledgements

Earlier versions of parts of these essays appeared in: *Critical Inquiry* 13:2 (1987), reprinted as *The Trial(s) of Psychoanalysis*, ed. Françoise Meltzer (Chicago: University of Chicago Press, 1988); *Discourse in Psychoanalysis and Literature*, ed. Shlomith Rimmon-Kenan (London and New York: Methuen, 1987); *Paragraph* 7 (Oxford: Oxford University Press, 1986); *Yale Journal of Criticism* 1:1 (1987). Grateful acknowledgement is made to the editors of these journals and collections, and to the publishers for permission to reuse the material.

Introduction

I have not been able to resist the seduction of an analogy.
Sigmund Freud, *Constructions in Analysis*

The publication of *Reading for the Plot: Design and Intention in Narrative* in 1984 established Peter Brooks as one of the foremost contemporary theorists of prose narrative. His two earlier books – *The Novel of Worldliness: Crébillon, Marivaux, Laclos, Stendhal* (1969) and *The Melodramatic Imagination: Balzac, Henry James, Melodrama and the Mode of Excess* (1976) – had already demonstrated his ability to provide sophisticated readings of individual texts and to raise important larger questions about, for example, the function of social relations or "worldliness" in eighteenth-century French literature or the need to reconsider the importance and influence of a scorned "popular" genre such as melodrama. *Reading for the Plot* resembles Brooks's earlier books in that it examines a number of prose fictions in order to explore and develop a larger thesis about literature: in this case, the fundamental congruence between modern literature and Freudian psychoanalysis and the implications this mutually illuminating relationship has for the study of narrative plot. His newest book, *Body Work*, continues to develop this focus on the relationship between literature and psychoanalysis, shifting our attention, as Brooks points out in his introduction to *Body Work*, from "a dynamics of desire animating narrative and the construal of its meanings" to "the objects of desire," specifically the sexualized human body. The first lecture in this book addresses the analogy between reading and erotic pleasure, and the essays included in general connect the concerns of *Reading for the Plot* with those of this most recent work.

Part of the lasting effect of *Reading for the Plot* is the result of its insistence on extending the stakes of this discussion of plot beyond mere literary formalism or traditional psychoanalytic criticism, both of which Brooks claims as precursors that are, in their older forms, unsatisfactory, too rigid, and even (in the case of earlier psychoanalytic criticism) "something of an embarrassment" (p. 20).[1] Both of these ways of reading, in their most reductive forms, tend to impose static "grids" or rigid structures of meaning on what Brooks insists are the dynamic processes through which narrative makes meaning and helps us impose meaningful order on the flux of temporal existence. By bringing a more dynamic narratology shaped by an emphasis on desire together with a more "textual and rhetorical" (p. 22) understanding of psychoanalytic criticism, Brooks suggests a more eclectic and productive approach to the development of form in modern narrative, supplementing the necessary but limited terminology of narratology with the rich, and perhaps more suggestive, language of psychoanalysis. The second part of this Introduction will address some issues implied in this development.

For the sake of better understanding Brooks's contributions to the study of narrative and psychoanalysis, we can isolate three major strands in his discussion of the nature and function of plot in prose narratives, none of which can be fully separated from the others:

1 an historical narrative, sometimes implied and sometimes explicit, that traces a movement in the nature

and function of plot in Western culture, from the earliest myths and tales to the fractured narratives of postmodernism;

2   a careful examination of Freud's psychoanalytic practice and formulation of a "masterplot" or paradigm for reading plot in narrative; and

3   close readings of prose narratives chosen to illuminate the various features of Brooks's argument in *Reading for the Plot*.

Part of the appeal and elegance of Brooks's work is the way in which these elements work together to create a synthetic, flexible model for understanding and discussing the dynamic processes of narrative. The stakes are indeed high in Brooks's meditation on narrative, for it is clear that he cannot imagine sustained thought without plot and sees narrative as a vital and necessary element of our lives, a psychic process in which we recognize and work through essential psychological needs for coherence and understanding.

Rather than viewing plot as a formula that inevitably ends up articulating a set structure, as in Propp's understanding of plot as a recombination of various relatively changeless syntactical elements, Brooks sees the narrative impulse as a more urgent attempt to cope with the human facts of our existence in the body and in time. He is acutely aware of the ways in which narrative helps us negotiate an unstable present through the counterpoint of hermeneutics and proairesis as "we engage the dynamic of memory and the history of desire as they work to shape the creation of meaning within time" (*RP*, p. xv). Plot becomes, for Brooks, kinetic rather than static, a desire machine designed and intended to adapt itself to the tensions inherent in the human condition, caught as we are between an often obscure yet powerful past wherein the origins of desire are buried, and a desired future that takes its shape from the past and present.

Implied in the argument of *Reading for the Plot* is an historical plot that takes us, in the nineteenth and twentieth centuries, "out from under the mantle of sacred myth" (*RP*, p. xii) and into a modern world in which narrative is scrutinized and destabilized, in which we have become both "suspicious of plots" – their artificial turnings and closings – and nostalgic for the order they seem once to have bestowed on our lives and cultures. Brooks's investigations of plot follow a generally chronological pattern, moving from tightly plotted narratives of closure and cure (fairy tales and detective stories, for example) to heavily plotted nineteenth-century novels such as *Great Expectations* to full-blown modernist narratives such as *Heart of Darkness* and *Absalom, Absalom!* The chapters of *Reading for the Plot* alternate between these readings of literary texts and considerations of theoretical issues raised by Freud's writings and clinical practice. Brooks's ability to oscillate creatively between theory and criticism and his application of theoretical insights gained from narratology and psychoanalysis to his articulate and productive readings of Balzac, Flaubert, Conrad, Faulkner, and others enrich his writing and allow him to develop an increasingly complicated argument about the "correspondence between literary and psychic dynamics" (*RP*, p. xiv). His theoretical speculations and his explorations of works such as Freud's *Beyond the Pleasure Principle* or Roland Barthes' *S/Z* suggest new ways of looking at such familiar texts as *Le Rouge et le noir, L'Education sentimentale, Great Expectations* or *Heart of Darkness*, and his readings of such texts in turn clarify his larger ideas about the nature of narrative.

The central thread that seems to run through Brooks's complex and inextricable web of narratology, psychoanalysis, the history of plot, and close reading is the connection between narrative and epistemology: an emphasis on story as a means of seeking knowledge and establishing truth. This interest in the relationship between narrative and truth connects *Reading for the Plot* with the lectures in this volume as well as Brooks's latest book, *Body Work*. In *Reading for the Plot*, the movements of memory and desire as they shuttle back and forth to uncover the origins of desire and to move toward the revelation or "full utterance" that we hope will come at the end or death of the plot,[2] the dialogic *Zwischenreich* or "intermediate region" (*RP*, p. 234) created by the transference, the breakdown of belief in plot – all partake of a need, even an instinct, for knowledge, for discovering the origins, development, and ends of the plots of our lives and our fictions. In *Body Work*, Brooks again turns to Freud for a central term in his argument: *Wisstrieb* or epistemophilia, the instinct for knowledge that arises, in Freud's "Three Essays on the Theory of Sexuality," from the child's desire to solve what Freud calls "the riddle of the Sphinx" – the mystery of where babies come from (*BW*, pp. 96–9). *Body Work* concerns itself with the desire to locate and uncover truth in or on the sexualized human body. The desire for knowledge and truth outlined in *Reading for the Plot* is generally less concerned with sexuality as both field and cloak for truth, though Brooks does align the motive narrative desire he discusses with sexual desire in an attempt to create what Susan Sontag has suggested could become "an 'erotics' of art" (*RP*, p. xv). On the whole, however, we find in *Reading for the Plot* a more generalized epistemophilia, a desire to uncover the past in order to move beyond the repetitions and returns that characterize middles for Brooks and move instead toward the desired end of narrative.

The history of modern plot that Brooks charts in *Reading for the Plot* mimics the movement of Freud's career, from his early confidence in the ability of psychoanalysis to discover the origins of neurosis and effect a cure to his growing sense that the truths reached in analysis were

more likely to be constructions than fact and that analysis might prove to be interminable. Brooks's debt to
Freud in *Reading for the Plot* extends primarily to two
complex notions, as Brooks points out at the end of his
book: "the energetic-dynamic model" adapts Freud's
discussion of the tension between the competing drives
of eros and thanatos in *Beyond the Pleasure Principle* into
a "masterplot" for narrative, while, on the other hand,
Brooks constructs "a model of the psychoanalytic transference as consonant with the narrative situation and
text" (*RP*, p. 320) from his reading of the Wolf Man case
history.

In the first of these central chapters, the widely anthologized "Freud's Masterplot: A Model for Narrative,"
Brooks examines narrative beginnings, middles, and
ends using Freud's *Beyond the Pleasure Principle* as a
paradigm for understanding narrative's "instinctive"
desire to seek its own cure in the death of plot, a death
that can only come – following the psychoanalytic model –
after the text has remembered and worked through its
own original and repressed secrets and traumas. Narrative middles repeat and replay lost time, delaying the
ending of the plot, in an attempt to gain a knowledge and
understanding of the relations of origins to desire and to
the ends of desire. Thus, in Brooks's reading of *Great
Expectations*, the novel begins with the loss or obscuring
of Pip's origins, identity, and name. Pip's confusion
about himself and his struggle to sort out inappropriate
plots and identities from his "true" self generates the
desire for knowledge that energizes Pip, the reader, and
the plot itself. Not until the past is mastered through
Pip's correct knowledge of himself can "this highly
plotted novel" (*RP*, p. xvi) reach its terminus.

The other model for reading narratives that Brooks
constructs from his reading of Freud is his suggestion of
psychoanalytic transference as a model for the working
out of a coherent narrative or *sjuzet* in response to an

incoherent *fabula*, an irretrievable primal scene. This model for narrative again foregrounds the desire to understand origins and the need to find a workable "truth," an explanation that will overcome narrative resistance and allow the "plot" – of one's life or one's fiction – to resume its movement into the future and toward its desired end. The most important focal point for Brooks's extensive discussion of the transference is Freud's Wolf Man case, treated at length in a chapter on the Wolf Man in *Reading for the Plot* and especially in his essay "Changes in the Margins: Construction, Transference, and Narrative" in this volume. Brooks's interest in the transference as a model for reading is reflected in his readings of Joseph Conrad's *Heart of Darkness* and William Faulkner's *Absalom, Absalom!*, modernist novels that reach similarly unsettling conclusions about the status of truth in narrative – its provisional nature, the impossibility of "full utterance," the inevitable obscurity of the past, and a modernist willingness to "settle" for a coherent narrative, an "incomplete, but not false, image of the universe" (*RP*, p. 318). In this model, plot and truth have become part of the transference – the negotiation of meaning between the analysand and the analyst, between the text and the reader, between one character and another – an attempt to *construct* a pragmatic, rather than empirical, truth. Thus Quentin and Shreve struggle, in *Absalom, Absalom!*, to recover and reconstruct the past in "a *necessary* hermeneutic fiction" (*RP*, p. 304; my emphasis). While in traditional prose narratives such as fairytales plot "works through the problem of desire gone wrong and brings it to its cure" (*RP*, p. 9), modernist and postmodernist narratives betray a deep suspicion of narrative "cure" achieved through formal closure. Faulkner's novel, like Freud's later writings, accepts the possibility that narrative (and analysis) can be interminable, but the need to know and understand, to find a "cure" for desire, and to construct a plot that will give order to the world is, as Quentin's compulsive desire to narrate demonstrates, as urgent as it ever was. Modernists such as Freud and Faulkner betray a nostalgia for plot that stands tragically against the modern awareness that "We have, in a sense, become too sophisticated as readers of plot quite to believe in its orderings" (*RP*, p. 314).

In using Freud's work as the basis for a masterplot for narrative, Brooks takes certain risks but also gains much in the way of an implied truth value and referentiality. The Freudian model of mind is of course now often viewed not only as arbitrary, but also as phallocentric, Eurocentric and ahistorical. Nonetheless, Brooks continues to depend on psychoanalysis, asserting his own "personal affinity with psychoanalytic thinking" (*BW*, p. xii), and continuing "to dream of a convergence of psychoanalysis and literary criticism because we sense that there must be some correspondence of literature and psychic process, that aesthetic structure and form must somehow coincide with the psychic operations they evoke, activate, appeal to."[3] As previously noted, by linking his own way of reading to Freud's, Brooks gains a model that mimics, in its own development from confidence to uncertainty, the historical narrative of plot that Brooks wishes to trace through modernism into postmodernism. Even more important, however, is the way in which the connection with psychoanalysis raises the stakes of his discussion of plot and suggests a sort of referentiality and reality through its focus on a textuality built out of the life stories of real individuals such as Dora or the Wolf Man. Torn between his desire to assert the anthropological importance – really, the possible *truth* – of psychoanalysis and his growing reluctance to privilege one term of the psychoanalysis/literature opposition over the other, Brooks has come to claim an intermediate or pragmatic truth value for the constructions arrived at through the psychoanalytic model of reading, a referentiality that he has come to qualify as "a certain referential function for narrative, where reference is understood not as a naming of the world, and not as the sociolect of the text, but as the *movement of reference* that takes place in the transference of narrative from teller to listener, and back again" (p. 72). Following Freud, Brooks sees that all "Attempts at seeing and knowing are attempts at mastering" (*BW*, p. 106), and, by extension, we can conclude that attempts to reach a final narrative truth, whether in psychoanalytic practice or in literature, are always of necessity attempts to master a reality and a temporality beyond our control. Perhaps, as Freud suggests, in his summing up of the Wolf Man case, "We must be content . . . with having clearly recognized the obscurity."[4] Within this model of narrative, memory and desire, reader and text, analyst and analysand work together dialogically in an effort to create, in an age of suspicion, narratives that may achieve a provisional but crucial truth, allowing us for a while longer to make meaning in the world.

John S. Rickard

Die Psychoanalyse war vor allem eine Deutungskunst.
Freud, *Jenseits des Lustprinzips*

In the opening paragraph of the third chapter of *Beyond the Pleasure Principle*, Freud announces that "twenty-five years of intense work" had made him realize that psychoanalysis was more than hermeneutics. The patient, asked "to confirm the analyst's construction," alas, never attained a conviction of the truth of any account of his repressions. Rather than remembering the unconscious "as something belonging to the past" (*ein Stück der Vergangenheit*), the patient was forced to repeat the unconscious in his present experiences. Freud's "*Stück der*

Vergangenheit" is the lost object of an art of interpretation, a *Deutungskunst*, thwarted by the suddenly complicated phenomenon of "present experiences." Not only is the past no longer "one piece," to which one may return at will, but the patient who would have pleased the doctor (*wie der Arzt es lieber sähe*) if he had remembered himself in the process, is thus cast into a state of perpetual dismemberment.

In the second of the three lectures of this volume, Peter Brooks quotes a case in point, Freud's infamous "Dora Case," which predates *Beyond the Pleasure Principle* by fifteen years. While formerly, as we have seen, Freud's psychoanalytic method had modelled itself on a more straightforward art of interpretation, that of Sherlock Holmes's logic of deduction, "Dora" illustrates the unforeseen complications Freud encountered in the transferential relation of the analyst with the patient. "Now the present itself is shown to be the place of struggle," as Brooks points out, and "What we thought at first to be a relatively straightforward . . . recapture of the past turns out to be something quite different" (p. 64). Indeed, the past under these changed circumstances is now "the story of the past" (p. 53) and "the analysand must eventually be led to a renunciation of the attempt to reproduce the past" (p. 53).

What is meant to be renounced here is the hypostasized past, the past as fact or fetish, from whose determinations psychoanalysis promises liberation – while attempting not to fetishize the cure itself. If not in fact, the cure must be in fiction, or not in "what was" but in "what might be," as Aristotle famously defined the difference between history and poetry, even to the extent that what might be, as Freud concedes, may be pure hallucination (p. 60). To mention Aristotle in the context of a fictive curative narrative recalls also Freud's enormous debt to the genre of tragedy itself. Like psychoanalysis, the form of tragedy, as Hannah Arendt insightfully points out, allows the protagonist to become "knowledgeable by re-experiencing what has been done in the way of suffering, and in this *pathos*, in resuffering the past, the network of individual acts is transformed into an event, a significant whole."[5]

Evidently Freud's case histories are modern tragedies, transformations of suffering into a narrative event, "a significant whole." Stanley Fish's discovery of a rhetoric of deception in Freud's case of the Wolf Man thus amounts to little more than a discovery of the necessarily rhetorical nature of the cure. "What might be" must inevitably be "what must be" – at least for the time being. Fish's attempt to expose a Freud dubiously entrenched in an imperious *Deutungskunst* out to establish nothing less than " 'unimpeachable fact,' "[6] simply neglects to read Freud's assertions of fact as necessary fictions. Moreover, these are fictions, as Freud's endless revisions intimate, that are consciously – Brooks thinks, heroically – entertained as such.

"In Brooks's reading," Fish explains, "the Wolf Man's case is a 'radically modernist' text, a 'structure of indeterminacy' and 'undecidability' which perilously destabilizes belief in explanatory histories as exhaustive accounts whose authority derives from the force of closure."[7] While Brooks, in an extended response to Fish, will staunchly reaffirm Freud's hermeneutics of indeterminacy, Brooks's own notion of the curative narrative construction nevertheless repeatedly stresses just those authorities of completion, closure, and force of conviction which Freud had allegedly left behind. Indeed, at first, and in certain fundamental assumptions, Brooks's theory does not depart too far from, say, John Crowe Ransom's advice to the aesthetically minded to "contemplate object as object," so as not to be "forced by an instinctive necessity to take it and devour it immediately."[8] With only minor differences, Brooks advocates "a tropology of the perversities through which we turn back, turn around, the simple consumption of texts, making their reading a worthy object of analysis" (p. 34). "Narrative truth," he declares, is "a matter of conviction, derived from the plausibility and well-formedness of the narrative discourse, and also from what we might call its force, its power to create further patterns of connectedness, its power to persuade us that things must have happened this way . . ." (p. 59). Fish's notion of the analyst's will to power, and perhaps as well the ideological implications of a formalist aesthetic, echo here audibly in Brooks's rhetoric of force and power. In spite of his advocacy of the transferential and therefore volatile and interminable nature of the talking cure, it bears initially all marks of a rhetorical construction demanding the coherence, force and completion formerly assigned to the aesthetic or to the explanatory histories and exhaustive accounts mentioned by Fish. Like the aesthetic, Brooks's "well-formed" narrative appears to seek refuge from the irreparable realities of history; it is a "special place," "an artificial illness," "the realm of the 'as if,' " "a special kind of present," a "symbolic replay of the past . . ." – all Freudian terms to which Brooks adds "a possible fiction to take the place of history" (p. 67). It is a fiction well exemplified in Balzac's story *Adieu*, where too literal an understanding of the past usurps the place of fiction, harming rather than healing the patient.

Brooks's aesthetic conception of psychoanalysis – emphasized by his insistence on the formal properties of narrative, its coherence, completion, and rhetorical force – leads necessarily to the admission that psychoanalysis is not really different from literature. Such an admission, however, now leaves open the possibility for a correspondence between the two discourses where neither is dominant. If literature and psychoanalysis relate to each other as an interplay, or as a catachresis, as Brooks proposes, both terms emphasize that neither fiction nor psychoanalysis is ground to the other, and that their positions of authority are interchangeable. The lack of a distinction between the literal and the figurative allows thus no judgement as to any truth value, and neither can psychoanalysis therefore have any explanatory power (p. 24); it takes place in the unverifiable twilight of Freud's transferential *Zwischenreich*. If this calls into question Fish's misgivings about Freud's alleged intentions, it also calls into question the legitimacy of psychoanalytical criticism itself. Brooks responds to such a charge that the sameness of structure, the cognitive and emotional correspondence between literature and psychoanalysis (p. 39), nevertheless reveals what he calls "the human stakes" (p. 35).

Brooks's claim hinges almost singly on his following of Freud's assumption that sexual desire and narrative plot, that erotics and aesthetic form are analogous, so much so that literature itself constitutes a fundamental part of human existence and that it would be advisable, Brooks suggests, to study precisely the form of literature, rather than the author or reader, or the fictive characters, if the human stakes were to be revealed. This amounts to an unexpected reversal of the usual argument that formal and aesthetic questions are gratuitous and indifferent to human affairs.

Given Brooks's aesthetic preferences, which lodge solidly in nineteenth-century realism, the dynamics of psychic processes seem to find their most fulfilling deployment in an aesthetic, with determinable beginning, middle and end, which offers (if only as a necessary fiction) the libidinal satisfactions of aesthetic closure. If "Dora" thus appears to Brooks as "a kind of failed Edwardian novel, one that can never reach a satisfactory dénouement" (p. 50), such a failure, one must hasten to say, seems inscribed in any narrative genre, even, as Freud's revisions of "The Wolf-Man" testify, in the various closures and hence in the perpetual openness of that narrative. Since a confirmation of narrative truth can thus only be established as "the illusion of creating a space of meaning" (p. 34), neither the denial nor indeed the patient's affirmation can, it seems, really terminate the analysis. Assertions such as "things must have happened this way," or "we must consider all narrative truth to be 'true' in so far as it carries conviction, while at the same time asserting that if it carries conviction it must in some sense be true" (p. 60) announce rather perilously, the absence of a ground of truth, and the necessarily circular epistemology of a narrative cure and psychoanalytic criticism. Neither psychoanalytic criticism nor the cure itself seem, therefore, to be immune from becoming themselves the mental disorder which Brooks discovers in the "faulty narratives" and which cause the patient to seek the counsel of the analyst. Hence the interchangeable roles of analyst and analysand or of reader and text.

Since modernism is contemporaneous with Freud's discovery of psychoanalysis, there is here then more than a coincidental resemblance between modernist texts and faulty narratives. The patient's story, "riddled with gaps, with memory lapses, with inexplicable contradictions in chronology, with screen memories concealing repressed material" (p. 47), resembles the modernist text, but so does the analyst's construction with its irony about its form and its anxiety about its readability. When Brooks generalizes these modernist characteristics, claiming an anxiety over transmittability even for the realist novel, this might ultimately mean that, in some degree, psychoanalysis itself must be included in the illness it seeks to cure.

Thus, Brooks will take us in his understanding of cure and narrative "beyond a formalist narratology" (p. 72). Rather than in the fetishizing of the aesthetic experience in a certain form and truth, and rather than as a "naming of the world" (p. 72), the cure takes place, like the reading of texts, "in the movement between text and reader" (p. 72). Rather than "the coherent, ordered chronological story," what is at stake is the process "in which narrative discourse orders story" (p. 55). The word for this process is the transference, perhaps the most fundamental of Freud's discoveries both for psychoanalysis and for the study of literature. It implies that the cure of mental illness, like the construction of a work of art, or like the interpretation of either, takes place neither in the present nor in the past, neither in the patient nor in the analyst, neither in the text nor in the reader. Its authority lies in its exchange, which is to admit also the indeterminacy of what constitutes that authority. "The truth of narrative is situational," Brooks concludes in his third lecture, "the work of truth reciprocal" (p. 101). The truth, like the authority of the analyst's constructions, is thus a self-conscious, interminable textual edition of the past, a story always under revision, always in transition between reader and text or between analyst and patient. Freud's interminable revisions of his past constructions may be the precursors of such a concept of narrative truth. Proceeding by addition rather than by substitution, Freud's texts exemplify the status of truth as endless text.

Thus, only in its dynamic interaction, in its dialogic form, or as Brooks claims – and this implies as well Freud's returns to his own texts – when the analyst "enters into the logic of [the patient's] symptoms" (p. 69) can the cure attain its coherence, force, and completion – although the claim for completion, for the terminable analysis that is also implied here, must appear under erasure. All the more so if it is largely the literary – that is to say, the interactive, transmissible, or scriptible nature of narrative, not the establishment of fact – that constitutes truth or mental health. Brooks quotes Freud to make the point that indeed the analyst proceeds by the same principle of interpretation as the modern reader of a text for whom an interpretation is likewise interminable: " 'The analyst . . . finishes a piece of construction and communicates it to the subject of analysis so that it may work on him; he then constructs a further piece out of the fresh material pouring in on him, deals with it in the same way and proceeds in this alternating fashion until the end' " (p. 56). But the end, as desired as it is impossible, seems ever delayed. "We have a feeling at the end of Marlow's narration," as Brooks writes about the epitome of modernist narrative, Conrad's *Heart of Darkness*, "that retelling of his tale will have to continue: that the ambiguous wisdom he has transmitted to his listeners will have to be retransmitted by them as narrative to future listeners" (*RP*, p. 260). "[I]n the last analysis," Brooks declares in the third lecture, "the desire for and of storytelling . . . subtends all other meanings, in literature as in the psychoanalytic transference" (p. 99).

Closure then, like aesthetic coherence and completion, is not in itself the cure, even if it is the motor of narrative, promising an eventual retrospective revelation of some – it would seem necessarily temporary – meaning of the story. Referring in his third lecture to Benjamin's celebrated essay "The Storyteller," Brooks points out that, for Benjamin, storytelling, understood as an oral, transferential relationship, will ultimately amount to an authentication of the reader's presence. Such a claim is, however, partially denied by Brooks: "we may not want to say, with Benjamin, that the reader encounters himself in this type of narrative" (p. 100). But why not? According to Brooks, "the reader must . . . come face to face with his inescapable desire for narrative, as the ultimate motivation of oral or written storytelling" (p. 100), and if this is true, then this desire seems to me to have its motivation in the reader's or patient's fundamental need to counteract his dismemberment with at least a symbolic form of presence – even if that presence can only be in language, the presence of an other.

One would insist then that the therapeutic quality of the transference resides precisely in the same qualities that make a literary text literary. And this may reemphasize the similarity between literature and psychoanalysis. For like the literary text, which (as Hans-Georg Gadamer has memorably pointed out) recovers the lost voice of writing by requiring an "always new, ideal speaking,"[9] psychoanalysis lastly reconfirms the presence of the analysand, reveals him – in his state of dismemberment – as the subject of a story, through which telling the patient might become (temporarily) whole – as whole at least as the story itself.

While the past resembles writing, psychoanalysis is the recovery of that writing through an always new, ideal speaking. Hence Benjamin's and Brooks's insistence on the interactive, dialogic nature of narrative. The analysand recreates himself as a fictional character in a story that "will never really be told. It can only be constructed, in the most conjectural manner" (p. 94). However, if it is "only" in the most conjectural manner, and in nothing more determinate than in a manner of conjecture that the difference of the present experience can be affirmed against the past, this might undermine Brooks's claim that psychoanalysis "believes in cure" (p. 71). If mental health cannot be established as fact, if the past is incurable, psychoanalysis can offer no cure. But what narrative conjectures, what the discourse of otherness can promise nevertheless, is treatment, a word that might intimate the interminability of psychoanalysis.

At least that much seems to me implied in Brooks's notion of Benjamin's oral storyteller, who appears as the ideal psychoanalyst, whose constructions necessarily include the listener and thereby assign the listener the role of correspondent in a structure of exchange impossible without his presence. I am not sure that such a "situational" or fictional ontology finally suffices to affirm the otherwise frail postmodern notion of subjectivity. But, in the absence of firmer, more determinate values – and Brooks's argument always returns to that absence – his narrative theory implies the importance of present (and this means interminable) social interactions. These now must replace both the final cure as well as the truth of the past. The Freudian subject, as Malcolm Bowie has pointed out, "is no longer a substance endowed with qualities, or a fixed shape possessing dimensions . . . it is a series of events within language, a procession of turns, tropes, and inflections."[10] Bowie's, like Brooks's, notions of subjectivity thus stress the enormous significance of keeping alive a humanistic tradition, or its narratives, which appear to be, alas, our only mode of being.

Harold Schweizer

REFERENCES

The following works by Peter Brooks are cited in the Introduction:

Reading for the Plot: Design and Intention in Narrative (Cambridge, Mass.: Harvard University Press, 1992) (*RP*)

Body Work: Objects of Desire in Modern Narrative (Cambridge, Mass.: Harvard University Press, 1993 (*BW*)

NOTES

1   Simple page references in this Introduction refer to Brooks's lectures in this volume.
2   Conrad, *Lord Jim*: "Are not our lives too short for that full utterance which through all our stammerings is of course our only and abiding intention?" Brooks uses this passage as the epigraph for *Reading for the Plot*.
3   "The Proffered Word," *Times Literary Supplement*, no. 4623 (November 8, 1991), p. 11.
4   "From the History of an Infantile Neurosis," in *The Standard Edition of the Complete Psychological Works of Sigmund*

Freud, ed. James Strachey (London: Hogarth Press, 1955), vol. 17, p. 105.

5   Hannah Arendt, *Men in Dark Times* (Harmondsworth: Penguin, 1973), p. 28.

6   Stanley Fish, "Withholding the Missing Portion: Psycho-analysis and Rhetoric," in *Doing What Comes Naturally* (Durham and London: Duke University Press, 1989), p. 545 and cf. p. 552.

7   Fish, p. 534.

8   John Crowe Ransom, *The World's Body* (Baton Rouge: Louisiana State University Press, 1938; repr. 1968), p. 44.

9   Hans-Georg Gadamer, *Wahrheit und Methode: Grundzüge einer philosophischen Hermeneutik*, vol. 1 (1960; reprinted Tübingen: J. C. B. Mohr, 1986), and *Ergänzungen/Register*, vol. 2 (1986), p. 353.

10   Malcolm Bowie, *Lacan* (Cambridge, Mass.: Harvard University Press, 1991), p. 76.

The Idea of a Psychoanalytic Criticism

If psychoanalytic literary criticism has been with us at least since 1908, when Freud published his brief essay, "Creative Writers and Daydreaming," the enterprise hasn't on the whole made a good name for itself. It's in fact most often been something of an embarrassment. The notion of psychoanalysis applied to literary study continues to evoke reductive maneuvers that flatten the richness of creative texts into well-worn categories, finding the same old stories where we want new ones. I find myself resisting the label "psychoanalytic critic" – though no doubt I am one, in some sense still to be defined – and worrying about the legitimacy and force that psychoanalysis may claim when imported into the study of literary texts. If the enterprise has recently been renewed in subtle ways by post-structuralist versions of reading, under the aegis of Jacques Lacan, a malaise persists, a sense that whatever the promises of their union, liter-ature and psychoanalysis remain mismatched bedfellows – or should I say, playmates.

The first problem, and the most basic, may be that psychoanalysis in literary study has over and over again mistaken the object of analysis, with the result that whatever insights it has produced tell us precious little about the structure and rhetoric of literary texts. Traditional psychoanalytic criticism tends to fall into three general categories, depending on the *object* of analysis: the author, the reader, or the fictive persons of the text. The first of these constituted the classical locus of psychoanalytic interest. It is now apparently the most discredited, though also perhaps the most difficult to extirpate, since if the disappearance of the author has been repeatedly announced, authorial mutants ceaselessly reappear, as, for instance, in Harold Bloom's psychomachia of literary history. The biographical continues to hold a perennial interest in our culture, and provides grounds for the deployment of psychoanalytic approaches, from the professional to the most amateur.

Like the author, the fictive character has been deconstructed into an effect of textual codes, a kind of thematic mirage, and the psychoanalytic study of the putative unconscious of characters in fiction has also fallen into disrepute. Here again, however, the impulse resurfaces, for instance in the moves of some feminist critics who want to show how the represented female psyche (particularly, of course, as created by women authors) refuses and problematizes the dominant concepts of male psychological doctrine. Gender-based criticism has in fact contributed to a new variant of the psychoanalytic study of fictive characters, a variant one might label the "situational-thematic": studies of Oedipal triangles in fiction, their permutations and evolution, of the roles of mothers and daughters, of situations of nurture and bonding, and so forth. Work of this nature can be methodologically disquieting in its use of Freudian analytic tools in a wholly thematic way – though this is of course part of its contestatory force – and in its implicit claim that the identification and labeling of human relations in a psychoanalytic vocabulary is the task of reading. The third traditional field of psychoanalytic literary study, the reader, continues to flourish in ever-renewed versions, since the role of the reader in the creation of textual meaning is very much on our minds at present, and since the psychoanalytic study of readers' responses willingly brackets the impossible notion of author in favor of the acceptable and also verifiable notion of reader. The psychoanalytic study of the reader may concern real readers (as in Norman Holland's *Five Readers Reading*) or the reader as psychological everyman (as in Simon O. Lesser's *Fiction and the Unconscious*). But like the other traditional psychoanalytic approaches, it displaces the object of analysis from the text to some person, some other psycho-dynamic structure, a displacement I wish to avoid since – as I hope to make clear as I go along – I think psychoanalytical criticism can and should be textual and rhetorical.

If the displacement of the object of analysis has been a major failing of psychoanalytic literary criticism, it has erred also in its inability to rid itself of the underlying conviction that it is inherently explanatory. The problem with "literature and psychoanalysis," as Shoshana Felman has pointed out more effectively than any other critic, lies in that "and."[1] The conjunction has almost always masked a relation of privilege of one term to another, a use of psychoanalysis as a conceptual system in terms of which to analyze and explain literature, rather than an encounter and confrontation of the two. The reference to psychoanalysis has traditionally been used to close rather than open the argument, and the text. This is not surprising, since the recourse to psychoanalysis usually claims as its very *raison d'être* the capacity to explain and justify in the terms of a system and a discourse more penetrating and productive of insight than literary critical psychology as usual, which of course harbors its own, largely unanalyzed, assumptions. As Simon O. Lesser states the case, "no 'common-sense' psychology yet employed in criticism has been helpful"; whereas psychoanalysis provides a way to explore "the deepest levels of meaning of the greatest fiction."[2]

Why should we reject such a claim? Even if psychoanalysis is far from being a "science" with the formal power of linguistics, for instance, surely certain of its hypotheses are so well established and so universally illustrated that we can use them with as much impunity as such linguistic concepts as "shifters" or "the double articulation." Yet the recourse to linguistic and to psychoanalytic concepts implies a false symmetry: linguistics may be universalistic, but its tools and concepts are "cool," and their overextension easily recognized as trivial; whereas psychoanalysis is imperialistic, almost of necessity. Freud works from the premise that all that appears is a sign, that all signs are subject to interpretation, and that they speak of messages that ultimately tell stories that contain the same *dramatis personae* and the same narrative functions for all of us. It is no wonder that Freud called himself a "conquistador": he extends remarkably the empire of signs and their significant decipherment, encompassing all of human behavior and symbolic action. Thus any "psychoanalytic explanation" in another discipline always runs the risk of appearing to claim the last word, the final hermeneutic power. If there is one thing that post-structuralist criticism has most usefully taught us, it is the suspicion and refusal of this last word in the interpretive process and history, the refusal of any privileged position in analysis.

The post-structuralist versions of psychoanalytic criticism have attempted to move out from the impasses of an inglorious tradition, to make psychoanalysis serve the study of texts and rhetoric rather than authors, and to stage an encounter of psychoanalysis and literature that doesn't privilege either term, but rather sets them in a dialogue that both exemplifies and questions how we read. The work of such critics as Felman, Neil Hertz, Leo Bersani, Sarah Kofman, Malcolm Bowie, Jane Gallop, Jacqueline Rose, Toril Moi – to give only a very partial list of those who have renewed the enterprise –

seeks to make the meeting of psychoanalysis and literature unsettling to both, a kind of interference of two systems productive of insight into each. Lacan's "return to Freud" in a trajectory through structural linguistics has pointed the way toward a rhetorical engagement of psychoanalysis and text. Lacan – not alone, but with the greatest panache and high-priestly drama – has taught students of literature to understand the basic operations of the "dream work," condensation and displacement, as the master tropes of rhetoric, metaphor and metonymy, reconfigured as fundamental psychic manifestations presented to analysis: symptom and desire – and thus to initiate a rereading of Freud attentive to his semiotic imagination, to the role of language as the medium of psychoanalysis and the structuring agent of the psyche.

But if we refuse to grant psychoanalysis any position of privilege in criticism, if we refuse to consider it to be explanatory, there may be reason to ask what we have left, and what its uses are. What is the status of a de-authorized psychoanalytic discourse within literary-critical discourse, and what is its object? If we don't accord explanatory force to psychoanalysis, what is the point of using it at all? Why do we continue to read so many critical essays laced with the conceptual vocabulary of psychoanalysis? What is *at stake* in the current uses of psychoanalysis?

I want to begin this inquiry with the flat-footed (and unfashionable) assertion that I believe that the persistence, against all the odds, of psychoanalytic perspectives in literary study must ultimately derive from our conviction that the materials on which they exercise their powers of analysis are in some basic sense the same: that the structure of literature *is* in some sense the structure of mind – not a specific mind, but what the translators of the *Standard Edition* of Freud's Works call "the mental apparatus" (*psychischer* or *seelischer Apparat*), a term which designates the economic and dynamic organization of the psyche, to a process of structuration. After all, it was Freud himself who readily admitted that "the poets and philosophers" had anticipated all he had to say. We continue to dream of a convergence of psychoanalysis and literary criticism because we sense that there ought to be, that there must be, some correspondence between literary and psychic process, that aesthetic structure and form, including literary tropes, must somehow coincide with the psychic structures and operations they both evoke and appeal to.

The belief in the possibility of such a correspondence of course depends on a more general belief, or intuition, that the psychoanalytic version of the human psyche is somehow "true," that it corresponds to one's own experiences and insights. Particularly, where aesthetics is concerned, it implies that the psychoanalytic view of humans as radically determined by sexuality has a general validity. By sexuality, I do not mean simple genitality, but rather large conceptualizations of the self as a sexual being, both deriving from and producing issues of gender difference, origins, and self-definition. Sexuality belongs not simply to the physical body, but to the complex of phantasies and symbolizations which largely determine identity. Sexuality develops as a swerve from mere genital utility, it is driven by infantile phantasies of satisfaction and loss, it involves a dynamic of curiosity which is possibly the foundation of all intellectual activity, as Freud suggests in his explorations of "epistemophilia," or the drive to know. Human desire emerges subject to the "laws" dictated by the castration complex and the Oedipal triangle – emerges, that is, as desire inhabited by loss and prohibition, which means that it is channeled by rules, including those of language, and subject to forms, including narrative plots. Human desire is from the outset always engaged in a struggle with trans-subjective forms and laws by which it is governed. And this may have something to do with our intuition that aesthetic form harbors an erotic force.

Part of the attraction of psychoanalytic criticism has always been its promise of a movement *beyond* formalism, to that desired place where literature and life converge, and where literary criticism becomes the discourse of something anthropologically important – where it teaches us something about the nature of human fiction-making, of both the banal everyday and the artistic sort. I very much subscribe to this urge, but I think that it is fair to say that in the case of psychoanalysis, paradoxically we can go beyond formalism only by becoming more formalistic. Geoffrey Hartman wrote a number of years ago – in *Beyond Formalism*, in fact – that the trouble with Anglo-American formalism was that it wasn't formalist enough.[3] One can in general indict Anglo-American "New Criticism" for being too quick to leap from the level of formal explication to that of moral and psychological interpretation, neglecting the trajectory through linguistics and poetics that needs to stand between. This was certainly true in traditional psychoanalytic criticism, which regularly short-circuited the difficult and necessary issues in poetics. The more recent – rhetorical and deconstructive – kind understands the formalist imperative, but I sense that it too often remains content with formal operations, simply bracketing the human realm from which psychoanalysis derives. Given its project and its strategies, such rhetorical/deconstructive criticism usually stays within the linguistic realm. It is not willing to make the crossover between rhetoric and reference that interests me – and that ought to be the *raison d'être* for the recourse to psychoanalysis in the first place. We need, I think, to make a psychoanalytically informed literary criticism serve to enhance an understanding of human subjects as situated at the intersection of several fictions created by and for them.

Daydreaming, Phantasy, and Narrative

One way to try to move out from the impasse I discern – or have perhaps myself constructed – might be through a return to what Freud has to say about literary form, most notoriously in the brief essay, "Creative Writers and Daydreaming" (1908). Recent psychoanalytic criticism has suggested that Freud speaks most pertinently to literary critics when he is not explicitly addressing art: such criticism has tended to draw more on *The Interpretation of Dreams*, the metapsychological essays, *Beyond the Pleasure Principle*, and the essay on "The Uncanny," for example, than on *Delusion and Dream*, *The Moses of Michelangelo*, or the essays on Leonardo and Dostoevsky. "Creative Writers and Daydreaming" in fact gives an excessively simplistic view of art, of the kind that allows Ernst Kris, in his well-known *Psychoanalytic Explorations in Art*, to describe artistic activity as regression in the service of the ego.[4] Yet the essay may be suggestive in other ways.

Freud sets out to look for some common human activity that is "akin to creative writing," and finds it in daydreaming, or the creation of phantasies. Freud then stresses the active, temporal structure of phantasy, which

> hovers, as it were, between three times – the three moments of time which our ideation involves. Mental work is linked to some current impression, some provoking occasion in the present which has been able to arouse one of the subject's major wishes. From there it harks back to the memory of an earlier experience (usually an infantile one) in which this wish was fulfilled; and it now creates a situation relating to the future which represents a fulfillment of the wish. What it thus creates is a daydream or phantasy, which carries about it traces of its origin from the occasion which provoked it and from the memory. Thus past, present and future are strung

together, as it were, on the thread of the wish that runs through them.[5]

Freud will promptly commit the error of making the past evoked in the construction of phantasy that of the author, in order to study "the connections that exist between the life of the writer and his works" (251) – an error in which most critics have followed his lead. For instance, it is this phantasy model, reworked in terms of Winnicott and object-relations psychoanalysis, that essentially shapes the thesis of one of the most ambitious studies in literature and psychoanalysis, Meredith Skura's *The Literary Use of the Psychoanalytic Process*; but Skura, too, ultimately makes the past referred to in phantasy a personal past, that of author or reader, or both.[6] Yet the phantasy model could instead be suggestive for talking about the relations of textual past, present, and projected future, in the plot of a novel, for example, or in the rhyme scheme of a sonnet, or simply in the play of verb tenses in any text. I would want to extrapolate from this passage an understanding of how phantasy provides a dynamic model of intratextual temporal relations, and their organization according to the plot of wish, or desire. We might thus gain a certain understanding of the interplay of *form* and *desire*.

Freud is again of great interest in the final paragraph of the essay – one could make a fruitful study of Freud's final paragraphs, which so often produce a flood of new insights that can't quite be dealt with – where he asks how the writer creates pleasure through the communication of his phantasies, whereas those of most people would repel or bore us. Herein, says Freud, lies the poet's "innermost secret," his "essential *ars poetica*" (153). Freud sees two components of the artistic achievement here:

The writer softens the character of his egoistic daydreams by altering and disguising it, and he bribes us by the purely formal – that is, aesthetic – yield of pleasure which he offers us in the presentation of his phantasies. We give the name of an *incentive bonus*, or a *fore-pleasure*, to a yield of pleasure such as this, which is offered to us so as to make possible the release of still greater pleasure arising from deeper psychical sources. In my opinion all the aesthetic pleasure which a creative writer affords us has the character of a fore-pleasure of this kind . . .(153)

I am deliberately leaving aside the end of this paragraph, where Freud suggests that the writer in this manner enables us "thenceforward to enjoy our own daydreams without self-reproach or shame," since this hypothesis brings us back to the *person* of the reader, whereas I wish to remain on the plane of form associated with "forepleasure."

The equation of the effects of literary form with fore-pleasure in this well-known passage is perhaps less trivial than it at first appears. If *Lust* and *Unlust* don't take us very far in the analysis of literary texture, *Vorlust* – fore-pleasure – tropes on pleasure and thus seems more promising. Forepleasure is indeed a curious concept, suggesting a whole rhetoric of advance toward and retreat from the goal or the end, a formal zone of play (I take it that forepleasure somehow implicates foreplay) that is both harnessed to the end and yet autonomous, and capable of deviations and recursive movements. When we begin to unpack the components of forepleasure, we may find a whole erotics of form, which is perhaps what we most need if we are to make formalism serve an understanding of the human functions of literature. Forepleasure would include the notion of both delay and advance in the textual dynamic, the creation of that "dilatory space" which Roland Barthes, in *S/Z*, claimed to be the essence of the textual middle, through which we seek to advance toward the discharge of the end, yet all the while perversely delaying, returning backwards in order to put off the promised end, and perhaps to assure its greater significance.

Forepleasure implies the possibility of fetishism, the interesting threat of being waylaid by some element along the way to the "proper" end, taking some displaced substitute or simulacrum for the thing itself, a mystification in which most literature deals, sometimes eventually to expose the displacement or substitution as a form of false consciousness, sometimes to expose the end itself as the false lure. Fetishism indeed seems to be characteristic of literature, perhaps especially of narrative literature in its "realist" phase, where objects, details, metonymies, and synecdoches predominate in the gradual creation of persons, places, and plots. As Freud explains in his essay on *Fetishism* (1927), the substitute or simulacrum comes to be invested with all the curiosity originally directed toward the missing object of investigation, the maternal phallus. The fixation of the fetishist on a certain object is comparable to "the stopping of memory in traumatic amnesia." Freud continues:

> As in this latter case, the subject's interest comes to a halt half-way, as it were; it is as though the last impression before the uncanny and traumatic one is retained as fetish. Thus the foot or the shoe owes its preference as a fetish – or a part of it – to the circumstance that the inquisitive boy peered at the woman's genitals from below, from her legs up; fur and velvet – as has long been suspected – are a fixation of the sight of the pubic hair, which should have been followed by the longed-for sight of the female member; pieces of underclothing, which are so chosen as a fetish, crystallize the moment of undressing, the last moment in which the woman could still be regarded as phallic. (*SE* 21: 155)

One could perhaps tease out the implications of this passage in conjunction with Roman Jakobson's celebrated insights on metonymy as the master trope of narrative. Fetishism might thus emerge as a key concept in narrative analysis because it accounts for the intense interest attributed to the detail or the accessory, read as signs of things to come, indices of character, investments of affect in things along the way, which must be valorized if reading is not to be a simple devourment of the text in order to reach its end.

Forepleasure includes as well the possibilities, related to fetishism, of exhibitionism and voyeurism, which surely are central to literary texts and their reading. Barthes indeed proposes the strip-tease as a model of reading, a progressive undressing or unveiling of meaning, through delays, feints, enigmas leading to false expectations before they are resolved. He introduces a specifically fetishistic notion when he asks, "Isn't the most erotic place of a body *there where clothing gaps*?" – the piece of flesh seen in the interstices of clothing.[7] Barthes sets such "gapping" in contrast to the strip-tease, where

> all the excitement is concentrated on the *hope* of seeing the genitals (the schoolboy's dream) or of knowing the end of the story (the novelistic satisfaction). Paradoxically (since it belongs to mass consumption), this pleasure is more intellectual than the other: it is an oedipal pleasure (to denude, to know, to learn the beginning and the end), if it is true that all narrative (all unveiling of the truth) is a staging of the Father (absent, hidden, or suspended) – which would explain the consubstantiality of narrative forms, family structures, and interdictions on nudity, all brought together in our culture in the myth of Noah's nakedness covered by his sons.

One may want to reject Barthes' sharp distinction between texts of strip-tease and of gapping, and to see both processes at work in the realist tradition of narrative, which promises an eventual disclosure, but works by way of partial and even unexpected uncoverings along the way. Access to the end – to fulfillment of desire, to knowledge of truth – usually is difficult and partial, it comes in glimpses and substitute revelations, in the accumulation of a displaced wisdom.

I don't intend to illustrate my general remarks through textual readings here. Let me simply cite, as a suggestive example, the moment from Flaubert's *Madame Bovary* when Rodolphe is leading Emma to the scene of their first lovemaking: "But her long riding dress got in her way, even though she held it up by the hem, and Rodolphe, walking behind her, fixed his eyes on the delicate white stocking exposed between the black cloth and the black boot, like a bit of nudity."[8] Rodolphe's voyeuristic forepleasure here figures the reading process in the novel itself, which always presents Emma Bovary as the fascinated object of gazes and consciousnesses that never take her in as a whole, but rather by way of fetishized accessories and features. We never see Emma in her entirety, which may suggest that she is not whole, that she is an incoherent bundle of desires – as her lovers and observers are inadequate registers of desire – but also may allegorize the status of the realist novel as a whole, which sets itself the task of knowing by way of phenomenal presence in the world, and thus limits its capacity to summarize and totalize. The novel offers an approach *to* much more than an arrival *at*.[9]

Narratives of approach that fetishize the objects of desire that they present, and thus tell the story of epistemological complexities that are also frustrations of desire, would offer a good field for investigation of how forepleasure structures the text, and becomes susceptible of great variety and complication. An example among many would be Barbey d'Aurevilly's *Le Bonheur dans le crime* (a tale from *Les Diaboliques*, another of which I discuss in chapter 3), where the principal narrator, Dr Torty, comes to scrutinize the very body of Hauteclaire Stassin for a sign of the crime that she and her lover have committed: poisoning her lover's wife. His inspection of her body fetishizes Hauteclaire as the woman who is impenetrable to the scientific gaze because she has no bodily opening. Torty says of the couple's unpardonable happiness after their crime: "You must believe that I have studied it well, scrutinized it well, rescrutinized it thoroughly! . . . I have put my two feet and my two eyes as much as I could into the lives of these two beings, to see if there wasn't in their astonishing and revolting happiness a fault, a crack, however small, in some hidden place."[10] Hauteclaire, the daughter of a master-at-arms who herself becomes a peerless fencer (and is named for the sword of Roland's companion Olivier), is commonly seen in the fencer's tights and jerkin, which become emblems of her impenetrability. The story thematizes fully a forepleasure which is at once sexual and cognitive, where indeed the quest for knowledge is both "scopophilic" and "epistemophilic," an erotically invested drive to see, to have, and to know, which constitutes the entire plot of the novella. Barbey, a belated Romantic who has reflected on the lessons of such as Balzac, Baudelaire, and Flaubert, gives notable versions of literature that is nothing but forepleasure: where knowing and having are so frustrated that all the drama is invested in approaches, overtures, voyeurism, and display.

In the notion of forepleasure there lurks in fact all manner of perversity, and ultimately the possibility of the polymorphous perverse, the possibility of a text that would delay, displace, and deviate terminal discharge to an extent that it became nonexistent – as, perhaps, in the textual practice of the "writeable text" (*texte scriptible*) prized by Barthes, in Beckett, for instance, or Phillippe Sollers. But we find as good an illustration of effective perversity in the text of Henry James, and in the principle (well known to the New Critics) that the best poems accommodate a maximum of ironic texture within their frail structures, a postponement and ambiguation of overt statement. In fact, the work of textuality may insure that all literature is, by its very nature, essentially perverse.

What is most important to me is the sense that the notion of forepleasure as it is advanced by Freud implies the possibility of a formalist aesthetic, one that can be extended to the properly rhetorical field, that speaks to the erotic, which is to say the dynamic, dimensions of form: form as something that is not inert, but part of a process that unfolds and develops as texts are activated through the reading process. A neo-formalist psychoanalytic criticism could do worse than attach itself to studying the various forms of the "fore" in forepleasure, developing a tropology of the perversities through which we turn back, turn around, the simple consumption of texts, making their reading a worthy object of analysis. Such a study would be, as Freud suggests, about "bribing," or perhaps about *teasing* in all its forms, from puns to metaphors, perhaps ultimately – given the basic temporal structure of phantasy and of the literary text – what we might call "clock-teasing," which is perhaps the way we create the illusion of creating a space of meaning within the process of ongoing temporality.

A more formalist psychoanalytic criticism, then, would be attuned to form as our situation, our siting, within the symbolic order, the order within which we constitute meaning and ourselves as endowed with meaning. This kind of psychoanalytic criticism would, of course, pay the greatest attention to the rhetorical aspect of psychic operations as presented by psychoanalysis, and would call upon the rhetorical and semiotic reinterpretation of Freud advanced by Emile Benveniste, Lacan, and others, and illustrated by the work of the best post-structural psychoanalytic critics. Yet it might be objected that this more obviously rhetorical version does not automatically solve the problem of how to use the crossover between psychic operations and tropes. The status of the "and" linking psychoanalysis and literary text may still remain at issue: what does one want to *claim* in showing that the structure of a metaphor in Victor Hugo is equivalent to the structure of a symptom? What is alleged to be the place and the force of the occulted name of the father that may be written in metaphor as symptom, symptom as metaphor?[11] Is there, more subtly now, a claim of explanation advanced in the crossover? Or is an ingenious piece of intertextuality all that takes place?

Something, I think, that lies between the two. My views on this question have been clarified by an acute and challenging review of my book, *Reading for the Plot*, by Terence Cave, that appeared in *TLS*. Cave asks what he calls "the embarrassing question . . . what is the Freudian model worth?"[12] In his discussion of a possible answer to this question, Cave notes that

> Brooks's argument for a Freudian poetics doesn't appear to depend on an imperialist move which would simply annex a would-be science of the psyche and release it from its claim to tell the truth. He talks repeatedly as if the value of the Freudian model is precisely that it does, in some sense, give access to the way human desires really operate.

I think this is accurate, and I am happy to be exonerated from the charge of imperialism in the reverse – the imperialism that would come from the incursion of literary criticism into psychoanalysis in search of mere metaphors, which has sometimes been the case with poststructuralist annexations of psychoanalytic concepts. I certainly do want to grant at least a temporary privilege to psychoanalysis in literary study, in that the trajectory through psychoanalysis forces us to confront the human stakes of literary form, while I think that these stakes need to be considered *in* the text, as activated in its reading. As I suggested earlier, I believe that we constitute ourselves as human subjects in part through our fictions, and therefore that the study of human fiction-making and psychic process are convergent activities, and superimposable forms of analysis. To say more precisely in what sense psychoanalysis can lead us to models for literary study that generate new insight, we might best look toward a concept that lies at the very heart of Freudian analytic practice, the concept of the transference, as it is constituted between analysand and analyst. Here we may find the most useful elaboration of the phantasy model of the text. This is, then, the model that I shall explore in some detail in chapter 2.

Psychoanalysis: Model or Metaphor?

But before turning to the transference, I need to say something more about the "status issues" involved in the meeting of psychoanalysis and literary study. It can be argued – and I have myself argued – that much of Freud's understanding of interpretation and the construction of meaning is grounded in literature, in those "poets and philosophers" he was the first to acknowledge as his precursors. "In which case," comments Cave in his review, psychoanalysis "can't itself provide a grounding, since it is part of the system it attempts to master." Cave continues: "Its advantage (though a precious one) would only be that, in its doubling of narrative and analysis, story and plot, it provides a poetics appropriate to the history of modern fiction." Cave here reverses the more traditional charge that psychoanalysis imperialistically claims to explain literature, to make the more subtle (and contemporary) charge that psychoanalysis may be nothing *but* literature, and the relations of the two nothing more than a play of intertextuality, or even a tautology.

Cave essentially argues that my uses of psychoanalysis, especially the concept of transference as a model for understanding the interaction of narrative between narrator and narratee, may really be more metaphor than model; and Mieke Bal has made the same point in her review of the book.[13] Cave's and Bal's criticisms suggest to me that there may be something to be gained by considering the differing status of the models and the metaphor, in an attempt to say which beast psychoanalysis imported into literary study really is. The critical and theoretical literature on metaphor is of course enormous, and that on models – especially in the philosophy of science – merely vast. But without exploring all possible definitions and analyses of the concepts, I think I can safely have recourse to Max Black's well-known study, *Models and Metaphors*, and mainly to the chapter in it entitled "Models and Archetypes," where Black precisely undertakes to consider the "value of recourse to cognitive models."[14] Black distinguishes among "scale models," "analogue models," and "theoretical models," which are generally continuous and share many common properties. In his terms, use of psychoanalysis in literary criticism – or of any other import from "the sciences of man" – would be first of all an "analogue model," comparable to hydraulic models of economic systems, for instance, in that it is called upon to provide symbolic representations of the original (i.e., literary texts) that are not simply reproductive, but homologous in structure. "The dominating principle of the analogue model," writes Black, "is what mathematicians call isomorphism . . . . The analogue model shares with its original not a set of features or an identical proportionality of magnitudes but, more abstractly, the same structure or pattern of relationships" (pp. 222–3). Psychoanalysis in literary study also has aspects of a theoretical model, which differs from the analogue essentially in that it "need not be built; it is enough that it be *described*" (p. 229). With both analogue and theoretical models, "Explicit or implicit rules of correlation are available for translating statements about the secondary field into corresponding statements about the original field" (p. 230). The analogue model easily slides into the theoretical model – a kind of hypothesis of intelligibility – when one considers how one translates from model to original: rather than simply thinking *by* analogy, one may – in the manner of a number of the great nineteenth-century English physicists, Clerk Maxwell or Lord Kelvin, for instance – think "*through* and by means of an underlying analogy" (p. 229). Even if one begins with the idea that the model is a heuristic fiction, there generally comes a moment of "ontological commitment" to the model, where "We pin our hopes on the existence of a common structure" in the model and its field of application.

What seems to be characteristic of the valuable model, then, is its force as a "speculative instrument" (to use a term of I. A. Richards' that Black cites with approval): the detailed and systematic consequences that result when one considers A in the light of a model provided by B, where systematic description of the structure of B should open new insights into the structure of A. Should this be taken to mean – in the case of psychoanalysis and literary study, for instance – that B provides a metalanguage for the analysis of A? The search for a metalanguage for literary study was of course a preoccupation of structuralist thinking in its early and most self-confident stage. Roland Barthes' attempt to construct a literary semiology, for example, testifies to this widely shared ambition to found a master discourse of literary discourse. Yet a post-structuralist Barthes, upon his inauguration of the Chair of Semiology at the Collège de France, would explicitly renounce this ambition, conceding that language can have no metalanguage.[15] In fact, use of models may be a way of avoiding the (impossible) notion of a metalanguage. As Black points out (citing R. B. Braithwaite's discussion in his book, *Scientific Explanation*), use of models avoids the " 'difficulties involved in having to think explicitly about the language or other form of symbolism by which the theory is represented.' "[16] Black indeed appears to set aside the notion of metalanguage when he speaks of an "analogical transfer of a vocabulary" between model and original, and when he argues that the "memorable models" of science operate in much the same manner as good metaphors: "They, too," he says of scientific models, "bring about a wedding of disparate subjects, by a distinctive operation of transfer of the *implications* of relatively well-organized cognitive fields. And as with other weddings, their outcomes are unpredictable. Use of a particular model . . . may . . . help us to notice what otherwise would be overlooked, to shift the relative emphasis attached to details – in short, to *see new connections*" (p. 237).

At this point, as Black admits, models come very close to looking like metaphors, which are "interactive" according to his definition, which is largely derived from I. A. Richards' definition, in *The Philosophy of Rhetoric*, of metaphor as a "transaction between contexts."[17] Both require "analogical transfer of a vocabulary"; like metaphor, a model may have "the power to bring two separate domains into cognitive and emotional relation by using language directly appropriate to the one as a lens for seeing the other." Nonetheless, Black is intent to maintain a distinction between models and metaphors. In the first place, he claims that the term *metaphor* is best restricted to relatively brief statements; the extended use of a model would find a more appropriate rhetorical analogue in the term *allegory*. More important, Black argues, is the fact that

> a metaphor operates largely with *commonplace* implications. You need only proverbial knowledge, as it were, to have your metaphor understood; but the maker of a scientific model must have prior control of a well-knit scientific theory if he is to do more than hang an attractive

picture on an algebraic formula. Systematic complexity of the source of the model and capacity for analogical development are of the essence. (p. 239)

Here, Black quotes Stephen Toulmin, in *The Philosophy of Science*:

It is in fact a great virtue of a good model that it does suggest further questions, taking us beyond the phenomena from which we began, and tempts us to formulate hypotheses which turn out to be experimentally fertile. . . . Certainly it is this suggestiveness, and systematic deployability, that makes a good model something more than a simple metaphor.[18]

Leaving aside for the moment Toulmin's somewhat dismissive notion of metaphor, I think we can safely claim that psychoanalysis on this definition does provide models to literary study. "Suggestiveness and systematic deployability" are precisely the characteristics that make us think that psychoanalytic models offer something of value to the literary critic. A number of suggestive models can be, and have been, systematically deployed in a way that effectively demonstrates the isomorphism of textual and psychic process. And like the theorists in physics whom Black admires, we consider this isomorphism to indicate not merely that the model is a good "heuristic fiction," but that it is existentially connected to its application, for this is how useful models generate understanding in their deployment. In other words, such models are not simply expository devices, illustrations; they are also discovery procedures.

What, in this context, might we say about Freud's understanding of his own use of models? Let me briefly cite two instances. In *An Autobiographical Study*, Freud describes the elaboration of his "topographical model" as an attempt "to picture the apparatus of the mind as being

built up of a number of *agencies* or *systems* whose relations to one another are expressed in spatial terms, without, however, implying any connection with the actual
anatomy of the brain" (*SE* 20:32). He goes on to say:
"Such ideas as these are part of a speculative superstruc-
ture of psychoanalysis, any portion of which can be
abandoned or changed without loss or regret the moment its inadequacy has been proved." Freudian meta-
psychology thus appears to be fully consonant with
Black's description of theoretical models in physics
which are held to be heuristic fictions but at the same
time are the object of an "ontological commitment,"
since we know that Freud thinks *in terms of* his topographical model, deploys it systematically so that it may
provide discovery procedures. My other example comes
from near the end of *Beyond the Pleasure Principle*, where
Freud offers an apology for the difficulty and the strange-
ness of the descriptions of psychic functioning he has
laid before his reader, and offers the explanation that the
apparent obscurity of the processes he has been present-
ing "is merely due to our being obliged to operate with
the scientific terms, that is to say with the figurative
language, peculiar to psychology." Freud continues:

> We could not otherwise describe the processes in ques-
> tion at all, and indeed we could not have become aware
> of them. The deficiencies in our description would prob-
> ably vanish if we were already in a position to replace the
> psychological terms by psysiological or chemical ones. It
> is true that they too are only part of a figurative language;
> but it is one with which we have long been familiar and
> which is perhaps a simpler one as well. (*SE* 18: 59)

The equation of "scientific terms" with "figurative language" (*Bildersprache*) appears effectively to abolish any
distinction between model and metaphor, to claim that
model is "merely" metaphor. Another set of scientific

terms might be preferable as a model because more familiar and possibly simpler, but it would be no less figurative. Freud thus explicitly admits – as Black only does implicitly – that model differs from metaphor only in its readier deployability and comprehensibility. Since Freud claims to be "obliged to operate" with a figurative language, the figure in question must in some manner be a catachresis, the kind of metaphor used to plug a gap in the signifying system. And catachresis is precisely the inescapable metaphor, that which allows of no distinction between "literal" and "figural," that which allows of no escape from the radically tropological nature of language.

Freud thus appears to be a more radical rhetorician than Black, to recognize that linguistic meaning depends radically on metaphor and the interaction of contexts. Now, the notion whose use as model or metaphor I will set out to elucidate – the notion of "transference" – is of course itself a representation, perhaps an allegory, of interaction or transaction. In the transference, the analysand constitutes himself as a subject by way of the dialogic and dialectic presence of the analyst, in a dynamic of erotic interaction. Furthermore, the whole relationship is metaphoric, in that it is based on the analyst's role as surrogate for past figures of authority, and the revival of infantile scenarios of satisfaction that are reproduced and replayed as if they were of the present. Freud repeatedly describes the transference as a realm of the "as-if," as an "artificial illness," and as a "new edition or reprint" of an old text. And of course, the word *transference* itself is merely the Latinate version of *metaphor*, as the German *Übertragung* is the Teutonic version. If I argue for a model of reading based on Freud's notion of transference, then, I use as model what is already a metaphor, or perhaps an allegory of metaphor. My doing so may suggest that the relationship I want to establish between psychoanalysis and literature is itself a transact-

ive and transferential one, based on a "transaction between contexts," to refer once more to Richards, and on
Black's "using language directly appropriate to the one
[domain] as a lens for seeing the other." What this may
come down to is an argument that the best – and perhaps
the only – model for the *use* of the psychoanalytic model
in literary study is the model of metaphor.

Students of literature should by now be convinced that
there is no metalanguage available to them. When critics
have taken psychoanalysis to be a metalanguage that
"explains" literature, they have always been talking
beside the point – the point being the structure and
rhetoric of texts. We must not, as Black says, use models
"metaphysically." But to say that the models available to
us in psychoanalysis are "only" metaphors should not be
a source of despair on an interactional, transactive, and
transferential understanding of metaphor. On the contrary, model as metaphor can in this view be "suggestive"
in its "systematic deployment," that is, can function as a
tool for both comprehension and discovery.

One can, then, resist the notion that psychoanalysis
"explains" literature and yet insist that the kind of inter-
textual relation it holds to literature is quite different
from the intertextuality that obtains between two poems
or novels, and that it illuminates in quite other ways. For
the psychoanalytic intertext obliges the critic to make a
transit through a systematic discourse elaborated to describe the dynamics of psychic process. The similarities
and differences, in object and in intention, of this discourse from literary analysis creates a tension which is
productive of perspective, of stereoptical effect. Psychoanalysis is not an arbitrarily chosen intertext for literary
analysis, but rather a particularly insistent and demanding intertext, in that mapping across the boundaries from
one territory to the other both confirms and complicates
our understanding of how mind reformulates the real,
how it constructs the necessary fictions by which we

dream, desire, interpret, indeed by which we constitute ourselves as human subjects. The detour through psychoanalysis forces the critic to respond to the erotics of form – that is, to an engagement with the psychic investments of rhetoric, the dramas of desire played out in tropes. Psychoanalysis matters to us as literary critics because it stands as a constant reminder that the attention to form, properly conceived, is not a sterile formalism, but rather one more attempt to draw the symbolic and fictional map of our place in existence.

NOTES

1 Shoshana Felman, "To Open the Question," *Yale French Studies* 55–6 (1977); reprinted Baltimore: Johns Hopkins University Press, 1982, pp. 5–10.
2 Simon O. Lesser, *Fiction and the Unconscious* (Chicago: University of Chicago Press, 1957), p. 297; p. 15.
3 Geoffrey Hartman, *Beyond Formalism* (New Haven: Yale University Press, 1970), p. 42.
4 See Ernst Kris, *Psychoanalytic Explorations in Art* (New York: International Universities Press, 1952).
5 Sigmund Freud, "Creative Writers and Daydreaming," *Standard Edition of the Complete Psychological Works* (London: Hogarth Press, 1953), 9: 147–8. Further references to Freud will be given within parentheses in the text, using the abbreviation *SE* for *Standard Edition*.
6 Meredith Skura, *The Literary Use of the Psychoanalytic Process* (New Haven and London: Yale University Press, 1981).
7 Roland Barthes, *Le Plaisir du texte* (Paris: Editions du Seuil, 1973), pp. 19–20; English trans. Richard Miller, *The Pleasure of the Text* (New York: Hill and Wang, 1975).
8 Gustave Flaubert, *Madame Bovary* (Paris: Gallimard/Folio, 1972), p. 215.
9 On these questions, see the more extensive treatment in my *Body Work* (Cambridge; Mass.: Harvard University Press, 1993), ch. 4.

10 Barbey d'Aurevilly, *Le Bonheur dans le crime*, in *Les Diaboliques* (Paris: Garnier/Flammarion, 1967), p. 164.
11 I allude here to an example used by Jacques Lacan in "L'Instance de la lettre," *Ecrits* (Paris: Edition du Seuil, 1966), p. 506ff.
12 Terence Cave, "The Prime and Precious Thing," *Times Literary Supplement*, January 4, 1985, p. 14.
13 Mieke Bal, "Tell-Tale Theories," *Poetics Today* 7: 3 (1986), pp. 555–64.
14 Max Black, "Models and Archetypes," in *Models and Metaphors* (Ithaca and London: Cornell University Press, 1962), p. 219. Future references to this essay will be given in parentheses in my text.
15 Roland Barthes, *Leçon* (Paris: Editions du Seuil, 1978), p. 36.
16 Black, p. 235. See R. B. Braithwaite, *Scientific Explanation* (Cambridge, 1953), p. 92.
17 See Black, "Metaphor," in *Models and Metaphors*; see I. A. Richards, *The Philosophy of Rhetoric* (New York: Oxford University Press, 1936), p. 94.
18 Stephen Toulmin, *The Philosophy of Science* (London: Hutchinson, 1953), pp. 38–9; cit. Black, p. 239.

Changes in the Margins: Construction, Transference, and Narrative

Stanley Fish has repeatedly mounted a strong argument that there are no grounds for interpretation that are not themselves the product of other acts of interpretation. Since there are no independent grounds of interpretation, there is no escape from rhetoric, meaning the discourse of persuasion, whose norms and constraints are set by the given community of interpreters. In an essay of his *Doing What Comes Naturally* entitled "Withholding the Missing Portion: Psychoanalysis and Rhetoric," Fish takes on that most interpreted and reinterpreted of Freud's texts, the case history of the "Wolf Man," arguing that Freud is simply engaged in a rhetorical power play, beating his patient, and his reader, into submission. Fish claims that Freud's elaborate construction of the Wolf Man's "primal scene" – the witnessing of his parents' copulation – is really "about" the "discursive power of which and by which it has been constructed."[1] That is, the unfolding of the Wolf Man's story really mimics Freud's own persuasive rhetoric. Freud finds what he needs, and orders it in dramatic fashion, in a narrative that has no basis other than its need to persuade.

In the course of the essay, Fish attacks my own reading of "The Wolf Man," in *Reading for the Plot* – where I found a kind of heroic honesty in Freud's exposure of his doubts about the reality of the primal scene – as a mistaken attempt to make Freud's text more "open," more "modernist," whereas he insists that it is a closed and totalitarian rhetorical performance. I don't want to defend my reading of "The Wolf Man" here. But Fish's essay does provide an opportunity to rethink Freud's narrative rhetoric. Essentially, Fish renews a traditional line of attack on psychoanalysis that claims that what the analyst finds is what he creates, that analytic interpretation is really "suggestion," and that the unfolding of the solution to the Wolf Man's case merely mirrors Freud's persuasive manipulation of the reader. I want to address these questions, not by way of the Wolf Man, and not so much directly, as by an argument concerning the grounds of narrative as a form of explanation and understanding, and Freud's specific contribution to our conception of narrative.

There appears at present to be increasing agreement, even among psychoanalysts themselves, that psychoanalysis is a narrative discipline.[2] As such, it at least implicitly displays the principles of its own "narratology." First of all, the psychoanalyst is ever concerned with the stories told by his patients, who are patients precisely because of the weakness of the narrative discourses that they present: the incoherence, inconsistency, and lack of explanatory force in the way they tell their lives. The narrative account given by the patient is riddled with with gaps, with memory lapses, with inexplicable contradictions in chronology, with screen memories concealing repressed material. Its narrative syntax is faulty and its rhetoric unconvincing. It follows that the work of the analyst must in large measure be a recomposition of the narrative discourse to give a better representation of the patient's story, to reorder its events, to foreground its dominant themes, to understand the force of desire that speaks in and through it. Finally, the kind of explanation in which psychoanalysis deals is inherently narrative,

claiming an enhanced understanding of the present –
and even a change in it – through histories of the past
that have been blocked from consciousness. As the histo-
rian Carlo Ginzburg has elegantly demonstrated, psychoanalytic explanation belongs to a long tradition of
narrative understanding that may reach back to the lore
of the huntsman, who deciphers and follows traces left
by his quarry – hoofprints, droppings, bent twigs and the
like – along a path that should lead to his goal: a form of
narrative explanation given its most obvious modern
realization in the classic detective story.[3]

Freud gives the psychoanalytic problem of narrative an
extended discussion in his first book-length case history,
the "Fragment of an Analysis of a Case of Hysteria"
(1905), better known by the name of its subject, "Dora."
He begins a treatment, Freud notes, by asking the patient for "the whole story of his life and illness," but that
is never what he receives. On the contrary: "This first
account may be compared to an unnavigable river whose
stream is at one moment choked by masses of rock and
at another divided and lost among shallows and sand-
banks." Freud continues in description of the patient's
narrative: "The connections – even the ostensible ones –
are for the most part incoherent, and the sequence of
different events is uncertain. . . . The patients' inability
to give an ordered history of their life in so far as it
coincides with the history of their illness is not merely
characteristic of the neurosis. It also possesses great theoretical significance." After explaining that amnesias and
paramnesias in the narrative serve the needs of repression, Freud concludes his preliminary discussion: "In
the further course of the treatment the patient supplies
the facts which, though he had known them all along,
had been kept back by him or had not occurred to his
mind. The paramnesias prove untenable, and the gaps in
his memory are filled in. It is only toward the end of the

treatment that we have before us an intelligible, consistent, and unbroken case history."[4]

Mens sana in fabula sana: mental health is a coherent life story, neurosis is a faulty narrative. Such a premise closely resembles that of the detective story, which equates the incomplete, incoherent, baffling story with crime, whereas detection is the making of an intelligible, consistent, and unbroken narrative. "Thus have you reasoned it all out beautifully in one long chain!" Watson exclaims to Sherlock Holmes, quite typically, at the end of one of their cases. The narrative chain, with each event connected to the next by reasoned causal links, marks the victory of reason over chaos, of society over the aberrancy of crime, and restitutes a world in which aetiological histories offer the best solution to the apparently unexplainable. We know that Freud was a student of Sherlock Holmes who perceived the close analogies between psychoanalysis and detective work.[5] It is not surprising that his earliest case histories, those of the *Studies on Hysteria* (1895), closely resemble the adventures of the London detective. In these early versions of "the talking cure," Freud at least implicitly claims that moving back from present symptoms, and the incoherent narrative offered in explanation of them, to the traumatic events and their subsequent revival in the patient's life, then the linking of events in an uninterrupted causal series, provides a narrative that is itself curative.

But Freud's understanding and practice of narrative would soon become much less straightforward, much more difficult and complex. The constitution of a present narrative in relation to the story of the past in Freud's practice becomes more complex and uncertain, the notion of causality more problematic; chronology itself is put into question by the workings of deferred action and retroaction; the part played by event and by phantasm becomes more difficult to unravel. What in particular makes the relation of narrative to the story of the past more problematic – hence more interesting for the narratologist – is Freud's progressive discovery of the transference, which brings into play the dynamic interaction of the teller and listener of and to stories, the dialogic relation of narrative production and interpretation.

"Dora" is in fact the key text of transition in Freud's understanding of narrative. "Dora" is the case history of an aborted analysis, and it reads as a kind of failed Edwardian novel, one that can never reach a satisfactory dénouement, and that can never quite decide what the relations among its cast of characters truly are: as if Freud were one of Henry James's baffled yet inventive narrators (as, for instance, in *The Sacred Fount*), but one who must finally give it all up as a bad business. What comes to complicate Freud's relation with his patient Dora, and thus also the case history he writes, is the workings of the transference, and Freud's discovery in the course of the analysis – but too late – that the relation of teller to listener is as important as the content and structure of the tale itself. Or rather: that the relation of teller to listener inherently is part of the structure and the meaning of any narrative text, since such a text (like any text) exists only insofar as it is transmitted, insofar as it becomes part of a process of exchange. Following the failure in the case of Dora, any narrative account will have to give a place to the transference, factor it in as part of the narrative situation.

As the discovery of the transference would complicate Freud's conception of narrative, so should it help us complicate, and refine, versions of narrative analysis that do not take account of the relations of tellers and listeners. It is my premise that most narratives speak of their transferential condition – of their anxiety concerning their transmissibility, of their need to be heard, of their desire to become the story of the listener as much as of the teller, something that is most evident in "framed tales" (such as Conrad's *Heart of Darkness*) which embed

another tale within them, and thus dramatize the relations of tellers and listeners. Narrative is always implicitly and often explicitly concerned with its channels of
communication, with what Roman Jakobson calls the
"phatic" function of language, its use to verify that the
circuits are open, as when we say on the telephone, "Can
you hear me?" Roland Barthes stresses that narrative is
always contractual, based upon an implicit or explicit
promise of exchange between teller and listener.[6] But the
model of contract is not entirely adequate. For what is at
stake is not only a relation of contract and obligation, but
as well the movement of something through the communicative chain, an act of transmission and reception.
Something is being transmitted or transferred from the
teller and is told to the listener, and to listening: it has
entered into the realm of interpretation. And if the story
told has been effective, if it has "taken hold," the act of
transmission resembles the psychoanalytic transference,
where the listener enters the story as an active participant
in the creation of design and meaning, and the reader is
then called upon himself to enter this transferential space.
It is here, I want to argue, that attention to Freud's discussions of the transference can help us to understand what
is at stake in narrative telling.

"Constructions in Analysis"

The most interesting text for our discussion is the late
essay of Freud's called "Constructions in Analysis"
(1937), an essay in which Freud rethinks the practice of
psychoanalytic narrative explanation. The essay displays
to a high degree Freud's awareness of the rhetoric of
psychoanalytic explanation. Indeed, in his opening paragraph, he notes that psychoanalysis has been accused of
operating on "the famous principle of 'Heads I win, tails
you lose' " (*SE* 23: 257) – the accusation renewed by

Fish, apparently without any awareness of Freud's explicit awareness of the problem. Freud concedes the apparent pertinence of the accusation, since "yes" and "no" are treated by psychoanalysis in a peculiar manner – often as equivalent – in relation to the confirmation or disconfirmation of interpretations. Freud thus sets out to "give a detailed account of how we are accustomed to arrive at an assessment of the 'Yes' or 'No' of our patients during analytic treatment – of their expression of agreement or of denial." The essay, then, concerns interpretation, persuasion, and re-formation of the patient's life story in the transferential space between analysand and analyst. In looking at it, I hope to gain some insight into the nature of psychoanalytic narrative explanation, and also to suggest how such explanation may offer a useful analogue to the critic concerned with literary narratives.

Like the contemporary essay "Analysis Terminable and Interminable" (1937), "Constructions in Analysis" represents a culmination of Freud's developing ideas on the transference. Many of the key concepts are expressed in two earlier pieces, "The Dynamics of the Transference" (1912) and "Remembering, Repeating and Working Through" (1914). Here, Freud presents a view of the transference as a special space created between the analysand and the analyst, one where the analysand's past affective life is reinvested in the dynamics of the interaction with the analyst. Freud in the latter essay writes:

> The transference thus creates an intermediate region [*Zwischenreich*] between illness and real life through which the transition from the one to the other is made. The new condition has taken over all the features of the illness; but it represents an artificial illness which is at every point accessible to our intervention. It is a piece of real experience, but one that has been made possible by especially favourable conditions, and it is of a provisional nature. (*SE*, 12: 154)

In other words, the transference is the realm of the "as-if," one in which the history of the past, its *dramatis personae* and emotional conflicts, becomes invested in a special kind of present, one that favors representation and symbolic replay of the past, and that should lend itself to its eventual revision through the listener's "interventions." Within the transference, recall of the past most often takes the form of its unconscious repetition, acting it out as if it were present: repetition is a way of remembering brought into play when recollection in the intellectual sense is blocked by repression and resistance. Repetition is both an obstacle to analysis – since the analysand must eventually be led to renunciation of the attempt to reproduce the past – and the principal dynamic of the cure, since only by way of its symbolic enactment in the present can the history of past desire, its objects and scenarios of fulfillment, be made known, become manifest in the present discourse. The analyst must treat the analysand's words and symbolic acts as an actual force, active in the present, while attempting to translate them back into the terms of the past. He must help the analysand construct a more coherent, connected, and forceful narrative discourse, one whose syntax and rhetoric are more convincing, more adequate to give an interpretive account of the story of the past than those that are originally presented, in symptomatic form, by the analysand.

Our sense that the transference, as a special "artificial" space for the reworking of the past in symbolic form, may speak to the nature of a narrative text between narrator and narratee – and eventually between authorship and readership – receives confirmation when Freud, in his discussion of what he failed to notice in time in the case of "Dora," calls transferences "new impressions or reprints" and "revised editions" of earlier texts (*SE* 7: 116). The transference is textual because it presents the past in symbolic form, in signs, thus as something that is "really" absent but textually present, and which, furthermore, must be shaped by the work of interpretation carried on by both teller and listener. As Jacques Lacan has insisted, the analyst by his mere presence – prior to any interpretive intervention he may make – brings to the analysand's discourse "the dimension of dialogue."[7] That is, if the transference necessarily elicits interpretation, it is equally true that the potential and the promise of interpretation, on the part of "the subject supposed to know" – the analyst – triggers the transference relation: the analysand's entry into the special semiotic and interpretive space of transference (which, I should add, very much includes the countertransference).

It is in "Constructions in Analysis" that Freud most explicitly addresses the distinct yet interactive roles played by analysand and analyst in the recovery of the story of the past in a present narrative. He makes clear early in the essay that his narrative ideal remains faithful to his earlier premises: "What we are in search of," he writes, "is a picture of the patient's forgotten years that shall be alike trustworthy and in all essential respects complete" (*SE* 23: 258). But he at once complicates the nature of this search by noting that the work of analysis "involves two people, to each of whom a distinct task is assigned" – the analyst and the analysand. Since the analyst has neither experienced nor repressed any of the story under consideration, his task cannot be to remember anything. "What then is his task?" asks Freud, to answer: "His task is to make out what has been forgotten from the traces which it has left behind or, more correctly, to *construct* it" (258–9). At this point, "construction" is glossed as "reconstruction," but the latter term will quietly disappear from the essay. Construction/reconstruction is likened to the work of the archeologist – in one of Freud's favorite and recurring analogies – since both archeologist and psychoanalyst "have an indisputed right to reconstruct by means of supplementing and combining the surviving remains": a remark we may already find suggestive of the relation between interpretive narrative discourse and the story it attempts to reconstitute. But there are differences, since in the case of psychoanalysis one can claim that every essential of the past has been preserved, "even things that seem completely forgotten are present somehow and somewhere, and have merely been buried and made inaccessible to the subject" (260). Indeed, what the psychoanalyst is dealing with "is not something destroyed but something that is still alive," since, as we know, his material consists in large part in "the repetitions of reactions dating from infancy and all that is indicated by the transference in connection with these repetitions" (259). That is, the "text" presented by the analysand contains in raw form everything that will be needed for its interpretive construction, a premise familiar to the literary interpreter as well.

As Freud's essay proceeds, "construction" becomes a radical activity. Consider his comment that "the time and manner in which [the analyst] conveys his constructions to the person being analyzed, as well as the explanations with which he accompanies them, constitute the link [*Verbindung*] between the two portions of the work of analysis, between his own part and that of the patient" (259). If this "link" still bears some resemblance to the Sherlock Holmesian chain of events, emphasis now has shifted from the chain itself – the coherent, ordered chronological story – to the way in which narrative discourse orders story – that is, the link between telling (including listening) and told. Narrative discourse takes shape between story (that which it claims to retrieve and to represent) and narrating (the telling that is productive of narrative discourse). The coherently shaped narrative places us, in the words of Paul Ricoeur, "at the crossing point of temporality and narrativity."[8] In other words, for Ricoeur as for Freud, the narrative is not simply "there," waiting to be uncovered or disclosed. On the contrary, narrative comes into being only through the work of interpretive discourse on story, seen as the raw material – what Freud in this essay calls *Rohstoff* – which becomes coherent and explanatory only as the narrating orders it in discourse. If we wanted to pursue the Sherlock Holmes analogy, we would have to look to those moments where the detective conveys to the criminal a hypothetic construction of events, to receive confirmation in the form of confession or self-betrayal. Yet we shall see in a moment that the confirmation of constructions in analysis entails a more complex narrative model.

The "link" of narrative discourse to story events in analysis is itself far from simple, since it does not take place at once, in a single uninterrupted operation. It works intermittently, interruptedly, in a dialogic manner. "The analyst," writes Freud, "finishes a piece of construction and communicates it to the subject of analysis so that it may work on him; he then constructs a further piece out of the fresh material pouring in on him, deals with it in the same way and proceeds in this alternating fashion until the end" (260–1). In such alternating, reciprocal work – *Abwechslung* – the analyst is always in the process of constructing narrative, forming hypotheses of interpretation and meaning, in the manner, indeed, of any listener to a story, or any reader with a text. Such an active, "constructivist" role for the analyst of course raises the possibility of "suggestion," of the imposition of false constructions on the analysand. What confirms that the analyst's constructions are correct? It is a well-known psychoanalytic dictum that the patient's "no" is unacceptable at face value, since it may likely be the denegation of "yes," the product of resistance. But "yes" itself has no value, says Freud, "unless it is followed by indirect confirmations, unless the patient, immediately after his 'Yes,' produces new memories which complete and extend the construction" (262). Evidently the only confirmation one can have that the narrative has been correctly constructed and construed lies in the *production of more story*. As readers, for instance, we know that our hypotheses of construal are strong and valuable when they produce in the text previously unperceived networks of relation and significance, finding confirmation in the extension of the narrative web. The process of listening to a story or reading a text is essentially constructive, a filling-in of gaps, a building of fragments into a coherent whole: a conquest of the non-narrative by the narrative, of non-sense by the semantic. And the measure of success in the constructive process is not so much in any assent that the text may give: a simple "yes" is of limited value unless it leads to a further opening up of the text, unless our constructions create further patterns of interconnectedness and meaning. And conversely, the "no" – Freud goes on to argue – may sometimes be read as an indication of incompleteness, a refusal to assent to a narrative construction that has not yet taken account of all the necessary story elements.

The view of narrative construction that appears to emerge from the model of psychoanalytic construction gives a large part to the role of the listener or narratee as dialogist in the creation of narrative and its meaning. As in most dialogues, the relation of teller and listener is simultaneously one of collaboration and struggle: collaboration toward the creation of the coherent and explanatory text, yet struggle over its interpretation and indeed over its very constitution, the elements of which it is made, their ordering, their shape. All of Freud's writings on the transference portray it as a realm and process of contest, over the lifting of repression and the mastery of resistances. In the case of "Dora," the analyst appears to gain his costly "victory" by too much imposing his construction of the text; while Dora makes the ultimate riposte available to the storyteller, that of refusing to tell further, breaking off before the end. "Constructions in Analysis," along with "Analysis Terminable and

Interminable," suggests that the analyst must learn to eschew such imposed solutions, that the collaboration and competition of the transference ultimately must put into question the privilege of the analyst. As with reader and text, there is no clear mastery, no position of privilege, no assurance, indeed, that the analyst and the analysand won't trade places, at least provisionally, and perhaps frequently.

The model of the transference indeed complicates any conception of interpretation as working from outside the text – as not implicated in its production. Shoshana Felman notes the peculiar place of the analytic reader when she argues that the profession of literary criticism allows one "not to choose" between the roles of analyst and analysand, because of the "paradox" that: "1) the work of literary analysis resembles the work of the psychoanalyst; 2) the status of what is analyzed – the text – is, however, not that of a patient, but rather that of a master . . . the text has for us authority – the very type of authority by which Jacques Lacan indeed defines the role of the psychoanalyst in the structure of transference." For to the analytic reader, the text is "a subject supposed to know" – it is, says Felman, "the very place where meaning, and *knowledge* of meaning, reside. With respect to the text, the literary critic occupies thus at once the place of the psychoanalyst (in the relation of interpretation) *and* the place of the patient (in the relation of transference)."[9] In fact, I would add, the reader shuttles between these places, in an unstable dynamic.

Even Freud's – and our own – common-sensical assumption that the analysand/storyteller, rather than the analyst, must in some ultimate sense "possess" the true story, which needs to be construed and put into proper form, will be complicated if we follow the implications of Freud's argument. For Freud notes that while "the path that leads from the analyst's construction ought to end in the patient's recollection," this is not always the case. "Quite often we do not succeed in bringing the patient to recollect what has been repressed. Instead of that, if the analysis is carried out correctly, we produce in him an assured conviction [*sichere Überzeugung*] of the truth of the construction which achieves the same therapeutic result as a recaptured memory" (265–6). Thus we learn that parts of the story of the past may not ever be recalled by the person whose story it is, or was, but may nonetheless be *figured* in a construction of them by the analyst-narratee – a construction which is unsubstantiated, unverifiable, yet carries conviction. Such "conviction" is no doubt the aim of any storyteller, as of any reader who tries to retransmit the experience of a text – when, in particular, as critic the reader tries to convince other readers that the construction of a given text *must be* right.

Narrative truth, then, seems to be a matter of conviction, derived from the plausibility and well-formedness of the narrative discourse, and also from what we might call its force, its power to create further patterns of connectedness, its power to persuade us that things must have happened this way, since here lies the only explanatory narrative, the only one that will make sense of things. Calling upon Lacan as a gloss to Freud, one could say that narrative truth depends as much on the discourse of desire as on the claims of past event. The narrative discourse – like the discourse of analysis – must restage the past history of desire as it exercises its pressure toward meaning in the present. The past never will be recollected at all except insofar as it insists on continuing to mean, to repeat its charge of affect in the present. And if the analyst – like the reader – must translate this insistence back into a coherent story of the past, he can do so only by working with the present remains of that story, reconstructing in such a way that the *re*-quietly drops out – as it does from Freud's essay –

to become simply, and more radically, construction, working toward the goal, not of verifiability, but of conviction: toward "what makes sense."

In the last pages of his essay, Freud moves to a discussion of delusions, similar to hallucinations, produced in the analysand by the analyst's constructions: delusions that evoke a "fragment of historical truth" that is out of its rightful place in the story, to which the analyst must bring a kind of syntactic correction.[10] Freud writes at this point, in quite an astonishing sentence: "The delusions of patients appear to me to be the equivalents of the constructions which we build up in the course of an analytic treatment – attempts at explanation and cure" (268). It appears that the interpretive analytic construction and the patient's delusional construction are "equivalent," two sides of one dialogic process, two versions of narrative that test themselves against one another, together working toward the construction of the "complete" and satisfying narrative text. Not only does the patient, in any successful analysis, become his own analyst, the analyst also becomes the patient, espousing his delusional system, working toward the construction of fictions that can never be verified other than by the force of the conviction that they convey. That Freud goes on in the very last paragraph of the essay to broaden his subject to the delusions of mankind as a whole, delusions which "owe their power to the element of historical truth which they have brought up from the repression of the forgotten and primeval past," merely confirms that we must consider all narrative truth to be "true" insofar as it carries conviction, while at the same time asserting that if it carries conviction it must in some sense be true – true to the experience of the past, which can of course be the experience of fantasy (as with the primal scene or scenarios of the primal horde) just as well as what we usually call fact.

Stories are told for purposes, to establish a claim on the listener's attention, an appeal to hearing, which is also an appeal to complicity, perhaps to judgment, and inevitably to interpretation and construction. In the transferential situation of hearing or reading, as in the analytic transference, the work of the reader is not only to grasp the story as much as possible, but to judge its relation to the narrative discourse that conveys it, seeking to understand not only what the narrative appears to say but also what it appears to intend. As Freud says in "Remembering, Repeating and Working Through," it happens that the analysand "does not listen to the precise wording of his obsessional ideas" (*SE* 12: 152). As we know most explicitly from modernist and postmodernist narratives – but it is no doubt true of all narrative – a certain suspicion inhabits the relation of narrative discourse to its story, and our role as readers involves a finely tuned and skeptical hearing, a rewriting of the narrative text in collaboration and agonistic dialogue with the words proffered by the narrator. Texts, like analysands, offer resistances, which must be progressively semanticized. And in fact, interpretation discovers that resistance is incorporate with its task, a factor in that struggle for mastery which, like repetition, both conceals and reveals.

Transferential Stories

It is clear that our, and Freud's, original model of narrative, in the detection narratives of Sherlock Holmes, has by now undergone considerable complication: complication by the interpretive presence of the listener, by the situation of transference which represents an uneasy dialogue between narrator and narratee, a struggle to construct and to control the text, and to master the past through its telling and interpretation in the present. It may be significant that the Sherlock Holmes canon contains at least one tale that in itself represents such a complication, and that it is a complication that it was in the logic of the canon eventually to produce. What I have in mind is "The Final Problem" – which at the time it was written (1893) was indeed intended to be the final Holmes story – where we find that the detective's work on London crime has both uncovered and produced Holmes's equal opposite, the "Napoleon of Crime," Professor James Moriarty, with whom Holmes becomes locked in "the most brilliant bit of thrust-and-parry work in the history of detection."[11] Holmes goes on, in words that anticipate Freud's talking about his particularly intelligent patient, Dora: "Never have I risen to such a height, and never have I been so hard pressed by an opponent." The essential point about Professor Moriarty is that his intelligence matches Holmes's: "he is a genius, a philosopher, an abstract thinker. He has a brain of the first order. He sits motionless, like a spider in the centre of its web. . . . You know my powers, my dear Watson, and yet at the end of three months I was forced to confess that I had at last met an antagonist who was my intellectual equal. My horror at his crimes was lost in my admiration at his skill" (172).

Moriarty's identity as Holmes's other, the necessary other of the transferential relation, is all the more strongly suggested in that Moriarty comes into being, as it were, through Holmes's own deductive powers, as a kind of structural necessity of the interpretive work of detection. It is as if Holmes's constant quest for crime to be detected had led to the establishment of a transferential situation in which finally he has his other, another "subject supposed to know" whose presence, even while invisible, will "dialogize" Holmes's words and actions in that they will always have to incorporate the reactions of the other. There is in fact a brief dialogue between Moriarty and Holmes, when the Professor visits Baker

Street to warn Holmes against continuing his pursuit, which follows an inevitable script since, as Moriarty says, "All that I have to say has already crossed your mind" (174). The more interesting dialogue takes place in the absence of the other, as Holmes and Moriarty deduce, tit for tat, what the other will do next, and act in response, in a manner of reasoning given its classic statement by Edgar Allan Poe's Inspector Dupin.[12] Thus, when Watson concludes that he and Holmes must have escaped Moriarty's clutches by catching the express boat train from Victoria Station, Holmes replies:

> "My dear Watson, you evidently did not realize my meaning when I said that this man may be taken as being quite on the same intellectual plane as myself. You do not imagine that if I were the pursuer I should allow myself to be baffled by so slight an obstacle. Why, then, should you think so meanly of him?"
> "What will he do?"
> "What I should do."
> "What should you do, then?"
> "Engage a special." (pp. 178–9)

Moriarty's "special" indeed roars by, shortly after Holmes and Watson have slipped off their train at Canterbury. And so it goes on. The tale unfolds as move and counter-move of detective and detected, with each in turn occupying each role, with each both pursuer and pursued, as in the unstable dynamics of the transference. The inevitable outcome is mutual extinction at the Falls of Reichenbach, where the "personal contest between the two men ended, as it could hardly fail to end in such a situation, in their reeling over, locked in each other's arms" (185).

In "The Final Problem," then, the logic of the detective narrative in its classic guise results in the creation of a new and putatively ultimate narrative which stages fully the dynamics of the transference. Here, as in "Constructions in Analysis," it is not only a matter of combining archeological fragments, or clues, into a narrative chain that links past and present and "solves" the problem of their interrelation. Now the present itself is shown to be the place of struggle and dialogue in the construction of a narrative that gives meaning to the past by writing its retrospective interpretation through the creation of its form. What we thought at first to be a relatively straightforward – albeit mentally and emotionally taxing – recapture of the past turns out to be something quite different: the effort, variously collaborative and agonistic, to construct, interpret, and control the past in the present. At issue, for both Freud and Sherlock Holmes in the revised models of their methods, is not so much the history of the past, or at least not the history of the past directly, as its present narrative discourse. This is the space of dialogue, struggle, construction. In the discipline and mastery of the transference lies the significant work of interpretation and understanding.

Turning from the detective story to other narrative modes, one could find the same principles at work in a number of narratives, especially those that dramatize the relations of tellers and listeners, and render the interpretation of the story told somehow difficult or problematic. I want to evoke briefly a tale of Balzac's that represents in notable ways the issue of construction. The tale I have in mind is *Adieu*, which recounts how Philippe de Sucy, out hunting near a friend's country estate, comes upon a deserted house lived in by a mad woman under the care of her uncle, a doctor. In the crazed young woman, Philippe recognizes with horror his long-lost love, the Comtesse Stéphanie de Vandières, whom he accompanied and protected during the retreat of Napoleon's army from Moscow, whose life he repeatedly saved, but from whom he became separated at the crossing of the infamous Berezina River, where he heroically commanded the building of a raft to bear her to safety, while he remained behind, to suffer years of enslavement in Siberia. The doctor takes over the narrative at this point, to inform Philippe's friend the Marquis d'Albon about the story of the past. He describes the banks of the Berezina on the eve of the final disaster of the French armies, when thousands of stragglers arrive at nightfall, exhausted and almost indifferent to their fate, and improvise bivouacs instead of crossing immediately on the pontoon bridge, which the commander of the rear guard then sets on fire at dawn, as the Cossacks descend. At the first passage of the Berezina, much of the Grand Army was destroyed; this second passage is a repetition in the mode of utter catastrophe, as thousands fall from the wrecked bridge into the water, thousands are crushed and killed by the melee, and the rest are made prisoner. The overloaded raft is launched, Stéphanie herself upon her arrival at the other side has lost her sanity. Following this traumatic moment, she wanders barefoot for two years in the wake of the army, and when the doctor finds her she can utter only the single word of her farewell to Philippe, *Adieu!* The doctor keeps her with another mad girl, working to "domesticate" her, as if she were a feral child, treating her with kindness but without any apparent progress toward a cure.

Once the doctor has finished his narrative of this horrific past moment shared, with such different results, by Stéphanie and Philippe, there begins a period of competition between Philippe and himself in therapy for Stéphanie. When the doctor dismisses Philippe as a meddler in his care of Stéphanie, Philippe conceives the project of a more radical kind of therapy, which will take the form of an attempted reconstruction of the scene of suffering and trauma, and then its repetition: one more crossing of the Berezina, a repetition of a repetition, another passage, an "artificial" one that will be the space of Philippe's "intervention," and is supposed to work his patient's cure. Reconstruction and repetition will in fact be literally based on a construction: the construction by Philippe of a representation of the Berezina River at the moment of its passage, eight years earlier.

Philippe retreats to an estate he owns in Saint-Germain, and spends the autumn in large-scale engineering projects. Working from a stream running through his grounds, he has workers dig a canal which will "represent the devouring river," builds and burns bridge trestles and bivouacs, and ravages his park "in order to complete the illusion on which he staked his last hope."[13] Then he orders ragged uniforms to clothe hundreds of peasants whom he engages to figure the French legions and the Cossacks. No detail is neglected in his search to "reproduce the most horrible of all scenes." Finally, "In the first days of the month of December, when snow had covered the ground with a thick white blanket, he *recognized* the Berezina" [my italics]. Philippe's "recognition" of the place of past trauma follows a series of terms that speak of reproduction and representation – "*représenter*," "*copier*," "*figurer*," "*compléter l'illusion*," "*reproduire*," – which culminates in the description of his constructed scene as a "représentation tragique." Notions of theatrical representation and psychic reproduction and repetition are very closely allied here: as in the "artificial illness" of the transference, we have a place of representation and reproduction where the past will be replayed in symbolic form, and in which the analyst will attempt to intervene in order to correct the sequel of the past, to rewrite its present consequences.

With the "recognition" of the scene of suffering by Philippe, the would-be analyst who is responsible for the construction, the stage is set for communicating the construction to the analysand, to see how it will work upon her. Early in January, 1820, Philippe dresses himself in the rags he wore on November 29, 1812, and has Stéphanie (temporarily drugged with opium) put back into her old clothes, then bundles her into a carriage similar to that which brought her to the banks of the Berezina. She now traverses "the fictive plain of the Berezina" (1011), and the staged drama begins: cannon thunders, a thousand costumed peasants howl in horror as the Cossacks descend upon them. Stéphanie jumps from the carriage and runs to the raft at the river's edge. As she stands before Philippe, her intelligence appears to come back to her: "she passed her hand over her forehead with the lively expression of someone who meditates, she contemplated this living memory, this past life translated before her, she turned her head quickly toward Philippe and *saw him*" (1012). The coloring and the freshness of a young woman spread across her face, her mind quickens. She speaks Philippe's name, and throws herself in his arms. But as he holds her, her body grows rigid. "Adieu, Philippe. Je t'aime, adieu!" she speaks in a weakening voice, and dies. The coda of Balzac's tale reports how Philippe, haunted by the memory of this tragic moment reproduced, doubled, eventually will commit suicide. "Construction" in *Adieu* is perfectly realized, literalized. It is forceful, persuasive, therapeutic, and also mortal. It is too good a fiction, in that its representational qualities take a fearsome toll in reality.

Such a toll is no doubt the negative or ironic version of the effect that any storyteller hopes to make on his listeners: stories ultimately seek to change the minds and the lives of those they touch. The analyst who makes constructions and communicates them to the analysand hopes to take a similar toll, to produce new confirming memories or else that "assured conviction" that allows a possible fiction to take the place of history, and to build a new narrative which ought to carry through to a new dénouement. The transference actualizes the past in symbolic forms so that it can be repeated, replayed, working though to another outcome, in a changed personal history. As I noted earlier, the transference represents that "intermediate region between illness and real life through which the transition from the one to the other is made." The transferential space is that margin – the place of fictions, of reproductions, of reprints, of repetitions – in which change is effected, through interpretation and construction. Freud writes in the final sentence of "The Dynamics of Transference": "For when all is said and done, it is impossible to destroy anyone *in absentia* or *in effigie*" (*SE* 12: 108). This statement may appear paradoxical, in that it is precisely "in effigy" – in the symbolic mode – that the past and its ghosts may be destroyed, or laid to rest, in analysis. If the past returns in the present, its identity with the past is, as Moustapha Safouan writes in his book on transference, "manifestly a matter of the signifier."[14] Freud is arguing, I believe, that the transference succeeds in making the past and its scenarios of desire relive in signs with such vivid reality that the constructions it proposes achieve the effect of the real. They do not change past history, but they rewrite its present discourse, and prepare an altered future. Such is no doubt the intention of any constructed narrative, as the case of Stéphanie and Philippe demonstrates in so exacerbated a form.

The ending of *Adieu* may remind us of the final moment of Shakespeare's *The Winter's Tale*, where the "statue" of Hermione, long reported dead as a result of Leontes" insane suspicions concerning her chastity, comes alive for the love of a repentant and long-suffering Leontes. She quickens in his embrace, in the manner of Stéphanie and Philippe, but with a different result. "Oh, she's warm!/If this be magic, let it be an art/Lawful as eating," exclaims Leontes. If it be magic in *The Winter's Tale*, it is white magic, with a happy outcome. Yet the play allows us to believe that it is not magic at all, but the happy end of a long process of working through that begins in Hermione's simulated death and ends in her fictive rebirth, in a scene constructed by Paulina when she feels Leontes has achieved the psychic and moral readiness necessary to the completion of his "cure." To describe the whole of the intervening action of *The Winter's Tale* in terms of the transference would be labored, and yet possibly suggestive, in that it offers a working through of the original problem – Leontes' jealousy and resulting erotic, epistemological, and moral insanity – in terms of other fictions, especially those of another generation, in Perdita and Florizel, that speak symbolically of the solutions available to the original problem and its actors. For our purposes, Shakespeare's play provides a useful foil to Balzac's tale, and provokes us to inquire more closely as to why Philippe's construction, albeit successful, provokes disaster.

Like Freud with Dora, Philippe too much imposes his construction of story and meaning, arrogating the position of the "subject supposed to know" without allowing a sufficiently interactive role for his patient. The doctor who has cared for Stéphanie before Philippe's arrival on the scene accuses Philippe of egotism and a misunderstanding of the therapeutic relation. This should be, not the constant demand for recognition and reciprocation that Philippe displays, but rather a long, patient self-abnegation and unhesitating devotion. The doctor understands and indeed enters into the logic of her symptoms, which Philippe would simply efface, eradicate. Philippe cannot abide Stéphanie's degradation as a woman, her lack of modesty, her failure to behave as the object of male desire. To which the doctor "acidly" replies, "What you wanted was madness as it is portrayed at the opera" (1009). The accusation is not unfounded: Philippe would no doubt prefer a scene from *Lucia di Lammermoor*, and his construction of the fictive crossing of the Berezina in his park indeed reminds us of the elaborate sets and machinery of grand opera. He puts too much faith in the capacity of representation and reproduction to carry the message of his drama. Stéphanie cannot but respond to the fidelity of the reproduction, but she is also crushed by it. She is given no place in the scheme, no position from which to speak herself, to enter into the dialogue of the transference. She is denied the possibility of counter-move that so characterizes Professor Moriarty in "The Final Problem" and that seems indispensible for the true work of construction. In attempting to exercise total control over the construction, Philippe violates the principle of the "alternating fashion" in which construction-building should proceed. He finally fails as a therapist, for himself as much as for Stéphanie. He reveals himself to be an imperfect reader, a rigid interpreter who fails to enter the delusional system of the text under consideration, who never understands the dialogic imperative. One cannot read, as one cannot cure, from the outside. It is only through assuming the burden and the risks of the transferential situation that one reaches the understanding of otherness.

What is at issue in psychoanalysis, Lacan says in his seminar on transference, "is nothing other than bringing to light the manifestation of the subject's desire." And what the subject desires, in the most general terms, is "the desirer in the other" ("*le désirant dans l'autre*"). The subject desires to "be called to as desirable."[15] For Lacan, the demand for love is always absolute, based on an unappeasable original lack, and desire is not desire for this or that, but desire *tout court*. So that the reciprocation of love becomes "giving what one does not have," a response produced from the "realm of non-knowledge." In this situation, the analyst must learn the "coordinates" needed to "occupy the place that is his, which defines itself as that which he should offer vacant to the desire of the patient in order for it to be realized as desire of the Other." The position of the analyst is thus one of renunciation, setting aside his own person to allow the analysand to listen to the echo of the desire he wants to

make heard. In entering the dynamics of the transference, the analyst renounces the totalitarian foreclosure of
interpretation and meaning.

To refuse or to fail to enter the transference is to
condemn oneself to reading always the same text, to a
solipsistic practice of interpretation. "It must change,"
as Wallace Stevens says of the supreme fiction. The
change that is wrought by fiction, as by psychoanalysis,
is a product of conviction: that a constructed narrative
makes sense of things. But to argue this is not to say, in
the manner of Stanley Fish, that the reader is hammered
into submission by a rhetorical power play. Fish can
write off "The Wolf Man" as an exercise in the rhetoric
of persuasion only, I think, because for him not much
appears to be at stake in psychoanalysis: the patient has
disappeared, only the reader is left. Whereas I want to
urge that the narrative constructed in psychoanalysis
finds its power of persuasion in its capacity to illuminate
the buried history of unconscious desire, to make sense
of an otherwise muddled life story.

What Fish's rhetorical version of psychoanalysis seems
to exclude is the possibility of change, of transformation,
through the transferential process. Fish appears to believe only in power, which has in fact become a central
idol much worshipped in recent criticism. Psychoanalysis, more humble and at its best more humane, also
believes in cure, by which it means the possibility of an
enhanced listening to the discourse of otherness, a new
reading of the history written by unconscious desire,
resulting in a changed understanding of narrative entail-
ments and consequences. The words of the analysand in
the psychoanalytic session form themselves in relation to
the listener. As Daniel Gunn says, in *Psychoanalysis and
Fiction*, "The power of the transference, like the power of
any love story, is rooted in the conjugating of these *two*
pronouns: 'you' and 'I.' "[16] The "I" and the "you," as we
know from Emile Benveniste's work on discourse, are

markers that change place according to who is speaking, in a relation that is necessarily dialogic. From this dialogue, even if it is asymmetrical – even if the analyst's commentary is largely marked by silence – arises the possibility for new understanding. In the transferential relation, there is a difficult, agonistic, and productive encounter. The same is true of the reading of texts, where we interpret, construct, building hypotheses of meaning that are themselves productive of meaning, seeking to understand narrative as both a story and the discourse that conveys it, seeking both to work on the text and to have the text work on us. Transference and construction suggest a properly dynamic model of narrative understanding that allows us to recapture, beyond a formalist "narratology," a certain referential function for narrative, where reference is understood not as a naming of the world, and not as the sociolect of the text, but as the *movement of reference* that takes place in the transference of narrative from teller to listener, and back again. It is in this movement of reference that change is produced – that the textual reader, like the psychoanalytic patient, finds himself modified by the work of interpretation and construction, by the transferential dynamics to which he has submitted himself. In the movement between text and reader, the tale told makes a difference.

NOTES

1 Stanley Fish, "Withholding the Missing Portion: Psychoanalysis and Rhetoric," in *Doing What Comes Naturally* (Durham and London: Duke University Press, 1989), pp. 525–54.
2 See, in particular, Donald P. Spence, *Narrative Truth and Historical Truth: Meaning and Interpretation in Psychoanalysis* (New York: Basic Books, 1984).

3 Carlo Ginzburg, "Spie: Radici di un paradigma indizia-
   rio," in *Miti, Emblemi, Spie* (Torino: Einaudi, 1986); English trans. John and Anne C. Tedeschi, "Clues: Roots of an
   Evidential Paradigm," in *Clues, Myths, and the Historical
   Method* (Baltimore: Johns Hopkins University Press,
   1989).

4 *Standard Edition of the Complete Psychological Works of Sigmund Freud* (London: Hogarth Press, 1953), 7: 16–18.
   Subsequent references to Freud will use the abbreviation
   SE, and will appear in parentheses in the text. The critical
   literature on "Dora" is very rich: see, in particular, Philip
   Rieff's "Introduction" to the case history (New York: Col-
   lier Books, 1963), pp. 7–20; and Steven Marcus, "Freud
   and Dora: Story, History, Case History," *Partisan Review*
   41: 1 (1974), reprinted in *In Dora's Case*, ed. Charles
   Bernheimer and Claire Kahane (New York: Columbia
   University Press, 1985), a volume which contains a number of other interesting essays on the case.

5 We are told of Freud's interest in Sherlock Holmes by his
   celebrated patient known as the "Wolf Man." See *The
   Wolf-Man by the Wolf-Man*, ed. Muriel Gardiner (New
   York: Basic Books, 1971), p. 146. For a further discussion
   of Holmes and Freud, see my *Reading for the Plot* (New
   York: Alfred A. Knopf, 1984; reprinted Cambridge, Mass:
   Harvard University Press, 1992), p. 269ff.

6 See Roman Jakobson, "Closing Statement: Linguistics and
   Poetics," in *Style in Language*, ed. Thomas Sebeok (Cam-
   bridge, Mass.: MIT Press, 1960), pp. 350–77; Roland
   Barthes, *S/Z* (Paris: Editions du Seuil, 1970), pp. 95–6;
   English trans. Richard Miller, *S/Z* (New York: Hill and
   Wang, 1975).

7 Jacques Lacan, "Intervention sur le transfert," *Ecrits*
   (Paris: Editions du Seuil, 1966), p. 216.

8 Paul Ricoeur, "Narrative Time," in *On Narrative*, ed.
   W. J. T. Mitchell (Chicago: University of Chicago Press,
   1981), p. 167. I use here the terms "story," "discourse," and
   "narrating" in the manner of Gérard Genette's *"histoire,"
   "récit," and "narration,"* referring, respectively, to the apparent order of events "as they happened" (the Russian Formalist *fabula*), the way they are presented in the narrative

(Russian Formalist *sjuzet*), and the productive act of telling. Though we tend to talk – as Freud does – of the "story" as primary, a moment's reflection allows us to see that it is in fact a derivative of the "discourse," the product of the reader's interpretation of a normalized chronology from what the narrative discourse gives us. See Gérard Genette, *Narrative Discourse* (trans. of "Discours du récit," in *Figures III*) (Ithaca: Cornell University Press, 1980).

9   Shoshana Felman, "To Open the Question," in *Literature and Psychoanalysis*, ed. Felman (Baltimore: Johns Hopkins University Press, 1982), p. 7.

10   On the notion of "historical truth," one must turn to *Moses and Monotheism* – which Freud was working on at the same time as the "Constructions" essay – to understand that it is contrasted to "material truth," truth substantiated by observable events or verifiable facts. "Historical truth" appears to have the same status as what he elsewhere calls "psychic truth": that which is true for the subject, whether its origins be real or phantasmatic, that which belongs to his understanding of his own story. Thus the opposition between "historical truth" and "narrative truth" argued by Donald Spence in *Historical Truth and Narrative Truth* seems to me fundamentally wrong: all of Freud's discussions put them on the same side of the antithesis, in opposition to "material truth."

11   Arthur Conan Doyle, "The Final Problem," in *The Adventure of the Speckled Band and Other Stories of Sherlock Holmes* (New York: NAL/Signet, 1965), pp. 172 and 173.

12   See Edgar Allan Poe, "The Purloined Letter": "But this ascendancy . . . would depend upon the robber's knowledge of the loser's knowledge of the robber" (it is the narrator speaking, then the phrase is repeated by Dupin); and the commentary on this passage by Jacques Lacan in his "Séminaire sur la lettre volée," *Ecrits*, p. 33ff.

13   Honoré de Balzac, *Adieu*, in *La Comédie humaine* (Paris: Bibliothèque de la Pléiade, 1976–81), 10: 1010.

14   Moustapha Safouan, *Le Transfert et le désir de l'analyste* (Paris: Editions du Seuil, 1988), p. 58.

15   Jacques Lacan, *Le Séminaire: Livre VIII: Le transfert*, ed. Jacques-Alain Miller (Paris: Editions du Seuil, 1991), pp. 234 and 414.
16   Daniel Gunn, *Psychoanalysis and Fiction* (Cambridge: Cambridge University Press, 1988), p. 217.

The Storyteller

Psychoanalysis, of course, is not only narrative and linguistic but also oral, a *praxis* of narrative construction
within a context of live storytelling. An exploration of the
transferential model of narrative meaning might profit-
ably think about the place of the oral within the written:
about the ways in which a literature which for a long time
has been thoroughly written and printed simulates, or
evokes, or carries traces of, the oral storytelling situation.
For it is in such a situation, however literarily elaborated,
that one may see the transferential properties of narrative
most evidently, most thematized, most patently part of
the textual structure. Next to the nineteenth-century
novel, which appears to be fully aware that it is a purely
bookish phenomenon, dependent on the new industrial
processes of printing and distribution, there are, for instance, tales – short stories and novellas – which often
insist, somewhat perversely, on their authentic relation
to a tradition and a communicative situation that are
clearly obsolete. If the familial and communitarian
gatherings which fostered the telling of the Tales of
Mother Goose and the *Kinder- und Hausmärchen* col-
lected by the Grimm Brothers – the evening watches
around the hearth which the French call "*veillées*" – may
survive in peasant culture in the nineteenth century, they
clearly have little to do with literature, which is in the

process of becoming commercial, even industrial, and, certainly in France, urban.

One can, for example, find in the work of Maupassant a notable instance of such an urban literature, self-consciously a commodity in a marketplace, which nonetheless returns again and again to fictive situations of oral communication. Maupassant's *contes* and *nouvelles* abound in examples of "framed tales," where one tale is embedded within another, where the storyteller of the embedded narrative speaks to someone in the outer frame who listens, where every narrator has one or more explicit narratees. What is at stake in these tales is often less the "message" of the story than its reception, less "what it says" than "how it communicates." To refer again to the terms of Roman Jakobson, at issue is perhaps less the "poetic" function of language than its "phatic" and "conative" functions: how, and by what means, the message is received, and with what results.[1] The tale told may represent an attempt at seduction, or even something close to rape, as in the rather sordid little tale called "Une ruse," where the ruse is not simply the theme of the story told by the doctor who has just been examining a newly wed woman, but also the ruse of narrating itself. When the young woman has listened to this fierce story of marital infidelity and dissimulation, she asks, now "tense" (*crispée*), "Why did you tell me this dreadful story?" To which the doctor, smiling, replies, "In order to offer you my services, should the occasion arise."[2] The "services" are of course rather shady ones, and their very offer constitutes a kind of violation of the newlywed, a forced loss of innocence. In other cases, the force of a narrative is such that it can provoke an interpretative discussion among its listeners (as in "Le Bonheur"), or the radical conversion of a whole life (as in "En voyage"). Narrating is never innocent, and the narrative that frames another allows the writer to dramatize the results of the telling. And this no doubt gives a signal to the reader that the tale told can and should react on his own life: that literature is not inconsequential.

One could at this point return to the *Decameron*, and to the whole literary tradition which insists that narrative implies narrating, which dramatizes a situation where a group of people is, for one reason or another, called upon to exchange stories. One could also evoke the picaresque tradition, where the chances of the highway ever lead to meeting new characters, who become characters precisely because of the stories they have to tell. These are what Tzvetan Todorov has baptized "narrative men" (*hommes-récits*): characters who exist to give birth to a new narrative, to a further structure of embedding in the narrative situation.[3] The ideal model of this genre would no doubt be *The Thousand and One Nights*, where one loses one's way in the attempt to follow the levels of embedding – tales within tales within tales within – which give the impression of a possible infinite regress, were it not that finally telling cures: cures the Sultan's murderous neurosis, provoked by his wife's infidelity, brings about the happy marriage of the Sultan with Scheherazade, and thus saves the state threatened by a parlous disequilibrium. Scheherazade knows perfectly well that narrating is never innocent, that telling a story can change a life. But what needs explanation, or at least exploration, is the survival of this oral tradition in the literary culture of the nineteenth century, and in texts that have nothing to do with the fantastic or the infantile, with the *veillée* or the circle of storytellers. Are we faced with a vestigial infancy of storytelling? Do we rather find a confirmation of the Bakhtinian notion that narrative discourse is always the meeting place of diverse voices? Or should we speak of a kind of nostalgia for a communicative situation that the modern writer will never experience?

I find it significant that the work of Balzac, the first novelist to be fully aware of the new conditions of an industrializing and commodified literature, very often stages situations of oral communication where the exchange and transmission of narrative is at issue. *Adieu* is of course an example – though one in which oral transmission is overshadowed by Philippe's literalist fictional construction – and there are many others, such as *Sarrasine, Facino Cane, Honorine.* But the most striking example might be *Autre étude de femme,* which presents a group of initiates gathered around the supper table of Félicité des Touches for a "second soirée" that follows the official reception, and which constitutes, in a few rare houses of the Faubourg Saint-Germain, "a happy protest by the ancient spirit of our joyous country."[4] It is thus under the sign of a preservation of the customs of the *ancien régime* in a new world where everything tends to "mechanize itself" – "se *mécanifer,*" in the words of the narrator – that several narratives are going to be offered by the members of this elite society, in a conversation "that has turned toward storytelling" (675). Each narrative constitutes a commentary on the one preceding it, and there are also explicit commentaries of the narratees, as well as unspoken but not unnoticed reactions of those who know themselves particularly implicated by certain narratives, but don't want it known. Here, says the narrator, narratives give us "secrets well revealed." This first narrator – who presents the gathering and for the moment remains anonymous – lingers in praise of the *salon* of Mlle des Touches, the most celebrated fictional novelist of *La Comédie humaine,* which he sees as a place for the true exchange of ideas: "here you will be understood, you will not risk staking gold pieces against counterfeit" (675). The exchange is one of real values. For here, "All eyes listen, gestures ask questions, and physiognomy responds." Here we have the summit of what he calls "the oral phenomenon." Over the course of the tale, we will discover that this first narrator who praises the exchange of stories is none other than Horace Bianchon, the famous doctor, the incarnation, in Balzac's world, of scientific method and objective observation. And it is Bianchon who will tell the final story of the evening, the most memorable, so much so that it has often been taken from its context and published separately under the title "La Grande Bretèche": a chilling drama of passion, dissimulation, and vengeance.[5] It is not without interest that this last story is told by the very person who presented the "theory," as it were, of oral communication, and that he manages to go beyond all the other stories of the evening, to create a sensation, and to gain the ultimate accolade accorded to the storyteller: that there is nothing left to say after he has finished, that the gathering breaks up, and the guests depart in silence.

We may detect in *Autre étude de femme*, as in so many other tales of Balzac, the desire of a novelist who has fully assumed the conditions of the modern professional writer – who indeed founded his own print shop in an effort to control the means of production of the written – to recover the oral context of narrative, to be in touch again with a lived situation of exchange between narrator and narratee, creator and public. At the same time, he assigns this oral context to a past which just barely survives in the modern world: it is seen as an anachronism, an object of nostalgia. One comes upon this nostalgia yet again – now in a highly nuanced and "modernist" form – in the remarkable essay by Walter Benjamin entitled "The Storyteller" (*Der Erzähler*), which merits our attention.

Storytelling and Wisdom

According to Benjamin, "the art of storytelling is coming to an end," which means that we are losing "the ability to exchange experiences": the very communicability of experience is threatened with loss.[6] From which it follows that "the art of storytelling is reaching its end because the epic side of truth, wisdom [*die Weisheit*], is dying out" (413; 87). Benjamin identifies traditional storytelling with the traveller, who returns from his wanderings with something to tell, but also with the preserver of local traditions, rooted in his native place. In the Middle Ages, these two types of storytelling interpenetrated because of the craft structure, whereby the resident master crafts-man and the traveling journeyman came together in the workplace. Benjamin writes: "If peasants and seamen were the old masters of storytelling, the artisan class was its university" (411; 85). But through the workings of "the secular productive forces of history," narrative has been taken from the realm of living speech, which now permits us to discover a new beauty in what is vanishing.

What stands in opposition to storytelling, what is in the process of replacing it entirely, is of course the novel, inseparably linked to the invention of printing and the notion of the book. For Benjamin – who is here closely following the Lukács of *The Theory of the Novel* – "The birthplace of the novel is the solitary individual, who . . . is himself uncounseled, and cannot give counsel to others" (413–14; 87). For the novelist is necessarily isolated, invisible, a hidden god who does not have the capacity to enter into colloquy with his fellow man, and thus cannot communicate that wisdom that is good counsel. Even more threatening to the survival of story-telling than the novel, according to Benjamin, is "informa-tion," the typical modern form of communication, the domain of the newspaper which, in providing expla-nations for everything, impoverishes our experience of narrative. Storytelling does without explanation and without psychological analysis, giving narrative a "chaste compactness" that commends it to memory and inte-grates it into the experience of the listener. It is in a state of relaxation, even a state of boredom (*Langeweile*) that the listener best assimilates the story told, makes it his own, in order to repeat it. As Benjamin writes in a quasi-Surrealist sentence, "Boredom is the dream bird that hatches the egg of experience" (417; 91). And this kind of boredom, already extinct in the cities, is dying out in the country as well. With it the "gift of listening" is disappearing, and the community of those who know how to listen. For, says Benjamin,

> storytelling is always the art of repeating stories, and this art is lost when the stories are no longer retained. It is lost because there is no more weaving and spinning going on while they are being listened to. The more self-forgetful the listener is, the more deeply is what he listens to impressed upon his memory. When the rhythm of work has seized him, he listens to the tales in such a way that the gift of retelling them comes to him all by itself. (417–18; 91)

For Benjamin, then, storytelling belongs to the world of the living world, the world of a communication that is authentic because it concerns the transmission and the sharing of experience, and that can thus become wisdom, the counsel of man to his fellow men. This wisdom, however, is less a factor of the "message" of the tale than of its integration in the storytelling situation: he is, once again, sensitive to the close ties among working, making, and telling:

> Storytelling as it long prospers in the realm of artisanry – the rural, the maritime, then the urban – is itself so to speak an artisanal form of communication. It does not aim to convey the pure essence [*an sich*] of the matter, like information or a report. It sinks the matter into the life of the storyteller, in order to bring it out of him again. Thus traces of the storyteller cling to the story the way the handprints of the potter cling to the clay vessel. (418; 91–2)

Benjamin's interest in Nikolai Leskov – the ostensible subject of his essay – may be explained most of all by Leskov's view (expressed in a letter that Benjamin quotes here) that writing "is for me no liberal art, but a craft [*ein Handwerk*]." Benjamin also cites a passage from Paul Valéry which evokes the imitation of the "patient process of Nature" in the accomplishment of perfect things – flawless pearls, well-aged wines – by the artisan in the making of "illuminations, elaborately detailed ivory carvings; hard stones perfectly polished and finely engraved; lacquer work and paintings realized through the accumulation of a number of thin, transparent layers."[7] Whereas today, "the time is past in which time did not matter. Modern man no longer works at that which can't be abbreviated."

It would appear thus far that we are faced with a fully nostalgic and romantic view of storytelling, one we may even judge to be utopian and mystified, especially when one considers that Benjamin is discussing a nineteenth-century writer who can at best give us a simulacrum of the "hand-made" story that would seem to be, for Benjamin as for Valéry, the only authentic illustration of his argument. One of the many difficulties presented by Benjamin's essay arises from his choice of an example which strikes us as an inauthentic instance of the matter under discussion. But this may be a signal that Benjamin is on the track of something that goes well beyond nostalgia, at least in any simplistic form. We need to pursue for another moment the meanders of his argument. He ends his quotation from Valéry with a sentence in which Valéry asks himself if the "increasing aversion to patient tasks" might not coincide with "a weakening in men's minds of the idea of eternity." And the idea of eternity, Benjamin adds, has its source in death. From which he will draw the conclusion that one might establish an equivalence in the changes – changes that are all losses – in the idea of eternity, in the figure of death, in the

communicability of experience, and in the art of storytelling. The idea of death itself is dying, according to
Benjamin, in that it has lost its public presence. "There
used to be no house, hardly a room, in which someone
had not once died," whereas modern man dies in the
hospital. Yet it is true that "not only a man's knowledge
or wisdom, but above all his real life – and this is the stuff
that stories are made of – first assumes transmissible
form at the moment of his death" (420; 94). Thus Benjamin can say, in a striking epigram, "Death is the sanc-
tion of everything that the storyteller has to tell."

I don't intend to pursue in detail all that derives, in
Benjamin's argument, from this primordial role assigned
to death as the authority of narrative. It is sufficient
perhaps to note that with the decline of the epic, memory
– the epic faculty *par excellence* – loses its original unity,
to become on the one hand "remembrance" (*Eingeden-
ken*), characteristic of the novel, and on the other "remi-
niscence" (*Gedächtnis*), characteristic of the story. For in
the novel, where according to Lukács the writer and the
reader are both solitary individuals, and where the essential and the temporal are radically separated, it is the
creative work of "active memory" that transforms everything, that confers on the struggle against time a certain
meaning. It is the "meaning of life" that is at the center
of any true novel. And since the meaning of a life is only
revealed at the moment of death, one reads a novel in
order to know death, that death that we will never know
in our own lives, that which, through the figuration of a
fictive life, gives us an image of what might constitute
meaning. The novel is significant, says Benjamin, "because this stranger's fate by virtue of the flame which
consumes it yields us the warmth which we never gain
from our own fate. What draws the reader to the novel is
the hope of warming his shivering life at a death he reads
about" (428; 101).

If it is thus the "meaning of life" which is at issue in the novel, we must on the other hand talk of the "moral of the story" – that is, of a participation and a sharing in wisdom between the storyteller and his listener. At the very end of his essay, Benjamin returns to the image of the flame: "The storyteller – he is the man who could let the wick of his life be consumed completely by the gentle flame of his story. This is the basis of the incomparable aura about the storyteller, in Leskov as in Hauff, in Poe as in Stevenson. The storyteller is the figure in which the righteous man encounters himself" (436; 109). The mention of Poe and Stevenson may well surprise us here, and leave us in some confusion concerning the historical coordinates of Benjamin's argument. But once again, we should understand that the apparent nostalgia of his evocation of the oral tale and its teller is in essence strategic: that he is not urging a return, even fictively, to a situation of storytelling which is gone for good (and which was perhaps always a myth), but rather waging a combat – whether in the advance guard or the rear guard it is hard to say – against the situation of any text in the modern world.

Anthropologists and linguists have taught us that in oral cultures, meaning depends in large measure on the context of any speech act. Writing, on the other hand, by its very nature abolishes context, to create an "autonomous discourse," a discourse that one cannot directly question or respond to because it is detached from its author and belongs, strictly speaking, to no one.[8] I detect in Benjamin's essay a protest against the decontextualization of discourse, and an effort to rediscover various coordinates of narrative, in narrative voice, in the transmission of a certain "wisdom" from narrator to narratee, in the transaction or transference that takes place every time that one recounts something to someone. Paradoxically, where it is a question of modern narrative, Benjamin's argument points the way less to an (impossible) return to the oral storytelling of the past than to a new attention directed toward certain aspects of the most highly elaborated textuality: to subtle signs of context in those texts that are the most self-conscious about their communicative situation and status. Our reading of Benjamin suggests that what may need to be scrutinized in narrative is less its "message," less its ostensible affirmations, and much more its interstices, its gaps, its moments of passage, the moments where something falls silent to indicate a transference, the moment where one begins to be able to hear other possible voices in response.

To pursue this line of thinking, we need to cite one further passage from Benjamin:

> A man listening to a story is in the company of the storyteller; even a man reading one shares this companionship. The reader of a novel, however, is isolated, more so than any other reader. (For even the reader of a poem is ready to utter the words, for the benefit of the listener.) In this solitude of his, the reader of a novel seizes upon his material more jealously than anyone else. He is ready to make it completely his own, to devour it, as it were. Indeed, he destroys, he swallows up the material as the fire devours logs in the fireplace. The suspense which permeates the novel is very much like the draft which stimulates the flame in the fireplace and enlivens its play. (427; 100)

We begin to understand that Benjamin's evocation of the sociable situation of storytelling, of the lived exchange that it implies, be it fictively – as simulated in and through the written – should be set in opposition to a situation of consumption of narrative in what he elsewhere calls "the age of mechanical reproduction." Benjamin is reacting against the aesthetics and the ethics of reading implied by the solitary consumption of the printed novel: against a reading that interiorizes and devours, that races like a flame through discourse the better to reach the signifying end. Lost in this kind of reading is the experience, or the illusion of the experience, of an exchange between living creatures, that human transaction which leads to reflection – and to reflexivity – and in its wake to wisdom, in the form of counsel given and received. What Benjamin would wish to restore, or to create, is perhaps most of all a certain attitude of reading that would more closely resemble listening, which would elicit the suspension of meditation rather than the suspense of consumption, and which would foreground the exchange, the transaction, even the transference – in a fully psychoanalytic sense – that can take place in the offer and the reception of a narrative. If Roland Barthes defined the nature of modern narrative as contract, Benjamin proposes rather the notion of narrative as gift: an act of generosity to which the receiver should respond by an equal generosity, either in telling another story (as in the model of the *Decameron* and its tradition), or in commenting on the story told, but in any event by the proof that the gift has been received, that the narrative has made a difference.[9]

If we return to our preliminary examples of the nineteenth-century oral in the written – Balzac's *Autre étude de femme*, Maupassant's "Une ruse" – we note that in fact the whole structure of embedding, the play of narrators and narratees, exists above all to verify and validate the reception of the narrative, to mark the difference that narrative makes. "Why have you told me this dreadful story?" asks the newlywed in "Une ruse." By indicating in this manner that she would have preferred not to hear the doctor's story, the young woman signals the modification that has been produced by the story. She will never again be as she was. Her listening to the story has produced a loss of innocence. Even if she will never need the doctor's "services" – even if she will remain faithful to her husband – the coordinates of her moral universe have been altered. In the knowledge of good and evil that she has acquired, however trivial it may be, there has been something of a fall. The transmission of narrative has cognitive value.

The attraction of nineteenth-century writers to situations of oral communication may be explained above all by their deep wish to believe in the cognitive value of narrative, its capacity to make a difference through the transmission of experience. This wish to believe might be the best starting point for a study of all that is deployed by modern narrative to signal, to underline, to dramatize the reception and the transmission of the narrated, and of narrative itself. This would of course be the moment to return to Jakobson's analysis of the six "functions" of language, to show how the study of those functions most often discussed in literary criticism – the emotive, poetic, and metalinguistic functions – needs to be completed by study of the conative and phatic functions, which concern reception and the channels of communication, and perhaps also study of the referential function, conceived not as the designation of an extra-textual referent but as that *movement* of reference that takes place in the exchange of narrative and the production of a modification. One should also introduce here Mikail Bakhtin's notion of "the dialogic," especially in the discourse of the narrator, to show how everything he says takes shape in relation to the possible, anticipated, imagined response of his narratee. For Bakhtin, the word is always implicitly in a situation of exchange: it never belongs wholly to the speaker, it is never virgin; it is always borrowed, and it carries with it the vestiges of all the other locutions in which it has already served. And of course it is here that one detects the pertinence of Freud's, and Lacan's, notion of the transference. For Lacan, we recall, the presence of the analyst as narratee always brings to the analysand's discourse, even without the overt intervention of the analyst, what he calls "the dimension of dialogue." If the transferential situation always implies the potential of interpretation, on the part of "the subject supposed to know" – the analyst – it is also the potential for interpretation that engenders the dynamics of the transference.[10] That is, the presence of a narratee-interpreter provokes a situation of transmission and transference, a situation which in its turn makes necessary the interpretative response of this narratee.

Narrative Ricochet

I don't intend to rehearse my discussion of these theoretical points of reference here, nor to attempt a direct "application" of the psychoanalytic concept to transference to a literary "reading." Rather, I want to discuss a narrative text against the background broadly painted by Freud and Benjamin, in their different modes, to see if the results may be suggestive. And rather than returning to Balzac or Maupassant, or moving on to Henry James – many of whose tales and novellas would furnish good examples of the effort to restore fictively the transferential situation of narrative (*The Turn of the Screw, In the Cage, The Beast in the Jungle* would all be prime examples) – I want to discuss a novella by Barbey d'Aurevilly, *Le Dessous de cartes d'une partie de whist*, one of the tales in his collection, *Les Diaboliques*. Like the other texts of *Les Diaboliques*, *Le Dessous de cartes d'une partie de whist* is highly "spoken": a first narrator in a Parisian *salon* dedicated to good conversation presents a second narrator, who will tell a story witnessed (though we will see that that word needs qualification) during his youth in a provincial Norman town, a story itself largely played out in a *salon*. This story will concern the arrival in the Norman town of a Scots gentleman, one Marmor de Karkoël, who achieves immediate acceptance and even celebrity because of his dexterity at the game of whist –

the unique passion of the bored local aristocracy – and who then apparently seduces the cold and seemingly chaste Comtesse du Tremblay de Stasseville, and possibly also her daughter Herminie, and maybe poisons both of them – or does the mother first poison the daughter? – before decamping for India. Both first and second narrator present their material in the digressive meanders of conversation, and with frequent appeals to the listener's (and the reader's) understanding and evaluation – that is, with repeated reminders that the speaker's monologue is presented in a situation of potential dialogue and transference.

The first narrator – let me call him the "outer narrator" – of this baroque and difficult narrative sets the scene, in the Parisian *salon* of the Baronne de Mascranny, which reminds us of Mlle des Touches' *salon* in Balzac's tale, since it, too, evokes an anachronistic survival of *ancien régime* conversational arts: "a kind of delicious Koblenz [Koblenz being the town in which many *émigré* French aristocrats gathered during the Revolutionary period] where the conversation of an earlier time found asylum, the last glory of the French spirit, forced to emigrate by the busy and utilitarian manners of our time."[11] This outer narrator is one of a circle of narratees who will listen to the embedded tale told by an *habitué* of the *salon* who is never named, but rather presented by way of his attributes:

> he was the most sparkling conversationalist of this kingdom of conversation. If that isn't his name, it's his title! Pardon. He had still another . . . Gossip or calumny, these twins who are so identical that one can't distinguish between them, and who write their gazette backwards, as if it were Hebrew (isn't it, often?), wrote in scratches that he had been the hero of more than one adventure that he certainly would not have wished to recount that evening. (176)

Already, there is a suggestion of a certain convergence
and interaction of narrative, the erotic, seduction, and
writing – writing of a difficult and inverted, perverse text,
one that we may have to un-read – a problematic suggestive of the transferential bond. The climax of the tale
comes when this "inner narrator" of the embedded
tale (what Gérard Genette would call the "intradiegetic"
narrator of the "metanarrative") himself becomes the
narratee of the old Chevalier de Tharsis (the inner-inner
narrator of the doubly embedded tale, in Genette's terms
the metadiegetic narrator of the meta-metanarrative),
who will tell him the "very obscure" story of the loves of
Marmor de Karkoël with the Comtesse du Tremblay de
Stasseville, and perhaps also with her daughter Herminie, who both die of apparent consumption a month
after Marmor's departure; and will tell him also about
the discovery, in a big flower box in Madame de Stasseville's drawingroom that was transplanted after her
death, of the body of an infant. But the Chevalier de
Tharsis cannot furnish a complete narrative: about the
dreadful story that must have been played out among
these characters, he can only provide "frightful conjectures" (217). Tharsis states his belief that the true underside of the cards is known only by Marmor himself, and
by the priest who was Madame de Stasseville's confessor.
But the inner narrator now replies that a woman of
Madame de Stasseville's impenetrable hypocrisy must
have died without confessing her sins: "The voice of the
priest broke against this impenetrable temperament, who
carried her secret off with her. If repentance had made
her confide in the heart of the minister of eternal com-
passion, one would not have found anything in the
planter of her drawingroom" (217). And at this point, the
inner narrator falls silent, and the outer narrator picks up
again, to recount the reactions of the group gathered in
the Baronne de Mascranny's *salon*, completing the framing

of the inner story told by the inner narrator, and the story within that, the one told by Tharsis.

In fact, the inner narrator thinks he knows more than Tharsis in some ways. If they were both witnesses to the famous scene of "diamond game" (about which more in a moment), and Tharsis was in fact one of the party of four whisters seated at the gaming table along with Madame de Stasseville, Marmor, and the Marquis de Saint-Albans, the inner narrator also witnessed, a fortnight before the "diamond game," Marmor in the process of pouring a subtle slow-acting poison into the interior of a ring with a concealed opening mechanism. It is impossible to know, however, whether this ring is identical to the diamond ring worn by Madame de Stasseville during the "diamond game," whether her own ring (if it is not the same as Marmor's) also is so contrived as to hold poison, and indeed whether there is any relation of cause and effect between the two scenes featuring rings, as between the two phenomena foregrounded during the "diamond game."

At this game, virtually at the same moment, the diamond on Madame de Stasseville's finger encounters a ray of sunlight and throws out "a dart of white fire so electric that it almost hurt the eyes, like lightning," while there is heard, coming from Herminie, "a horribly dry cough" (206). Two questions are posed, almost simultaneously, by Tharsis and by Saint-Albans: "Oh, oh! what's that sparkling?" and "And who is it that's coughing?" To these two questions, Madame de Stasseville replies in one sentence: "It's my diamond and it's my daughter." In her sentence, the connection between the two phenomena is made by way of the pure conjunction "and." It is impossible for us to say whether this "and" marks a connection of cause and effect, or whether it simply states a pure contingency. Moreover, if we accept the notion that a connection between diamond and cough has been established, we cannot determine whether this connection is effected purely on the plane of the signifier, as a rhetorical gesture, or whether it is motivated on the plane of the signified. Is this linkage of the diamond and the cough purely a verbal metonymy? Or is it a referential metonymy, so to speak? Can one in either case find adequate motivation for the move from the term "coincidence," used by the inner narrator (210), to the epithet "murderous jewel" (210) which he also uses? Are we, as in the detective story, faced with a clue, or are we rather dealing with coincidences, verbal contingencies, and fantasies? Ultimately, are we dealing with a narrative moment – which would imply connections of cause, or at least of consecutiveness – or with a kind of collage? The inner narrator himself confesses to be in doubt: "These facts, whose relation one to another I didn't see very clearly, these facts dimly illuminated by an intuition for which I reproached myself, in the tangled web of which the possible and the incomprehensible appeared, received later on a ray of light which forever clarified the chaos for me" (212). But we have already seen that this "ray of light," that which he will be given by Tharsis, is in fact quite dim and uncertain: if Tharsis is fully competent to count the three corpses that are the net result of this story, the story itself remains a matter of conjectures and gossip. Indeed, the cumulative knowledge of Tharsis and the narrator reposes on very fragile bases: each supposes that the other possesses some sure information that neither in fact has, and explanations are constructed without any convincing evidence. If at the end of the detective story the confession of the suspect often comes to confirm the hypotheses of the detective, here we have as a last conjecture the probability that Madame de Stasseville died without confession. One will thus never truly know the underside of the cards. The story promised by this narrative – or rather, by these narratives, in the plural – will never really be told. It can only be constructed, in the most conjectural manner.

These uncertainties may have the effect of sending us back to the end of the tale, to the moment where the outer narrator picks up the narrative, to close the outer frame. Here he first of all notes the relative failure of the inner narrator's narrative: "The storyteller had finished his story, this novel which he had promised, and of which he had only shown what he knew, that is, its outer edges [*les extremités*]" (217). But the very lack of completion of the tale told by the storyteller produces a certain effect of reception in its narratees: "Each listener remained wrapt in thought, and completed, with his own imagination, this authentic novel which he had to judge only by way of a few disparate details." We may be reminded of the end of Balzac's *Sarrasine*, where the narratee, Madame de Rochefide, "*resta pensive*": this "pensivity," not wholly susceptible to analysis and articulation, is the sign of the effect created by the tale told, of the need to process and absorb its transferential force. In both *Sarrasine* and *Le Dessous de cartes*, it is the active constructive work of the narratee, as of the reader, that is activated by the problematic story told. But since this work is characterized, in the *salon* of the Baronne de Mascranny, especially by silence (which marks "the most flattering of successes" for a narrator), we as readers again encounter a failure in our attempt to found an interpretation of the tale on the interpretations that it has provoked. The outer narrator, who upon entering the *salon* has slipped "behind the splendid velvety back of the Comtesse de Damnaglia" (175), is reduced to interpreting signs furnished by what we might consider to be the least expressive part of the anatomy: "What was expressed by the steely blue eyes of the comtesse? . . . I did not see them, but her back, touched by a light perspiration, had its physiognomy. It is said that, like Madame de Stasseville, the Comtesse de Damnaglia has the strength to hide many a passion and

many a pleasure" (218). It is said that (*On prétend que*) . . .
But finally one only sees the cards from the back, the
underside remains hidden.

Are we to conclude that Barbey's story is a kind of *jeu
d'esprit* that self-destructs in the complexities of its telling? Is it a version, in the orally imitative tale, of
Flaubert's novelistic ideal of a "book about nothing"? I
would not wish to accept so facile a conclusion. I would
suggest, rather, in the manner of the signs one sees at
French railway crossings: "*Attention*: *un récit peut en
cacher un autre.*" There may be another story hidden by
the apparent one. In the failure of the apparent story, *Le
Dessous de cartes* sends us back to the agency of narrating;
that is, to the communicative situation activated and
dramatized by the manner in which the narrative is
presented. Barbey's original working title for this tale
was "Ricochets de conversation," and it is in these ricochets, in the back and forth (recall Freud's *Abwechslung*)
between interlocutors, in the interstices of the told, that
the tale unfolds its other story. As the outer narrator
tells us, in his comments on the inner narrator's tone
and manner of presentation, this other story borders on
impossibility of representation: "But could I ever evoke
this narrative without diluting it, nuanced as it was by
voice and gesture, and especially could I ever bring out
the counterpoint of the impression that it produced on
everyone assembled in the sympathetic atmosphere of
that *salon*?" (178). Between the "point" of the story and
the "counterpoint" (*contrecoup*) of its reception is produced something that is perhaps more interesting than
what is actually said – or certainly more interesting than
what is said when it has assumed the form of the written.
One hears an echo of this situation in Freud: "It is well
known that no means has been found of in any way
introducing into the reproduction of an analysis the conviction that results from the analysis itself" (*SE* 17: 13).

If representation of the exchange, the transmission, the transference of the tale is strictly speaking impossible, since these take place in the interstices of the narrative discourse, in the dialectics of telling and listening, one can nonetheless specify to some extent the motivation of storytelling and its exchange. When he begins his tale, the inner narrator sets the scene of the drama he will evoke, a small Norman town which he calls "the most deeply and fiercely aristocratic of all France" (178), where the ruined nobility prefers its gradual extinction to the unsuitable marriage. The imagination of the narrator is especially obsessed by the young women of the nobility:

> The girls, ruined by the Revolution, were dying stoically old and virgin, leaning on those coats of arms that were their sufficiency against all need. My puberty was inflamed by the ardent reverberation of these lovely and charming young things who knew their beauty to be useless, who sensed that the wave of blood that beat in their hearts and tinged with crimson their serious cheeks boiled in vain. (179)

In this aristocracy, and especially in its maidens, there appears to be a sexuality that is all the stronger for its having to remain in a state of absolute repression. The very emblems of that repression are presented as bodily metaphors of the repressed, when, for example, the narrator evokes "the missionary crosses" that the maidens wear "on their budding bosoms," or the group of girls in the corner of a *salon*, "whispering at the most when they spoke, but yawning within so much that it reddened their eyes, and contrasting by their rather unbending posture with the supple grace of their figures, the pink and lilac of their dresses, and the wanton playfulness of their blond shoulders and their ribbons" (182). That which cannot be expressed through normal erotic rituals comes to be invested in card games. The narrator says: "the only thing that had, I won't say the physiognomy of a passion, but which at least was like movement, like desire, like the intensity of sensation, in this singular society where the maidens had eighty years of boredom in their limpid and untroubled souls, was gaming, the last passion of worn-out souls" (183).

Passion repressed thus invests itself in games, but also – this is stressed when one returns to the outside frame, to the Baronne de Mascranny's *salon*, that "delicious Koblenz of conversion," Parisian version of the *salons* of the Norman town – in storytelling. Instead of passion itself, the members of the *salon* will have a tale about passion (and we recall the description of the storyteller as a hero of the written-in-reverse gazette of gossip). Since the same repressed passion gives rise to both game and story, one is forced to consider the equivalence of these two activities, to see that the tale offered us closely resembles a game of whist, one of these four-handed games, with two sets of partners, where what counts is the exchange of cards, and perhaps most of all – the text dwells on this – the dealing of cards, at which Marmor shows himself to be an uncontested master. Now, in the games of whist played in the *salon* of the Marquis de Saint-Albans, there are exchanges of money, there are winners and losers. And yet, since the rubbers follow one another without interruption, day and night, and players relay one another, in the long run the game economy seems to reach a net result of zero. The game is played for the pleasure of playing, because it is the sole place for the investment of that eros that has no other place to go. The same can be said of storytelling. Stories are told for the pleasure of the telling, to give expression to a desire that otherwise would be condemned to a perpetual virginity.

It seems, however, that in the interstices of the games of whist, Marmor, Madame de Stasseville, and Herminie manage to lift the bar of repression and to reinvest in the erotic that which has been displaced into gaming – or perhaps rather to eroticize gaming to the point that it becomes the chosen place for a return of the repressed. At least, one can so surmise. Similarly, through the elegant playfulness of the narrative, with all its detours, its suspensions, its decoys, not only does the erotic work its way through toward overt expression, truth seems to make an appearance as well. Once again, this is particularly visible in the interstices of the narrative discourse, in the moments where narrating is interrupted, for instance after the reflection of the inner narrator that for certain souls there seems to be "a pleasure of imposture . . . that one plays a comedy for society, which is taken in by it, and one pays oneself back for the costs of this theatrical production by voluptuous sensations of contempt" (201). This exposure of the theatrical economics of dissimulation provokes among the narrator's female audience a "nervous shiver" that the outer narrator notices on the back of the Comtesse de Damnaglia. "Sometimes a shiver like this is called, poetically, *death going by*. Was it here truth going by? . . ." (202). What matters is perhaps less the nature of this truth – finally rather banal, like all the truths that concern passion – than its manner of being produced, as an effect of narrating, as a "shiver" that marks the transmission of narrative, that proves the transference is functional. As in the famous "diamond game" a link – whose nature is undecidable – was established between the sparkling diamond and the coughing girl, here there is the forging of a link – a "shiver" whose semantics may be fully as undecidable as in that other link – between the tale and its listening. One senses that a movement of reference has taken place between narrating and listening.

What can we conclude from this much too cursory reading of a tale which, from its very epigraph, warns us of its playful and deceitful nature ("Are you making fun of us, Sir, with such a story?" says the epigraph)? In introducing what he is going to recount, the interior narrator strikes a pose similar to that of many Balzacian narrators: "I who am speaking to you, I saw during my youth . . . no, 'saw' is not the word! I guessed, I sensed one of those cruel and terrible dramas that are not played out in public, though the public sees the actors every day; one of those *bloody comedies*, as Pascal used to say . . ." (177). The allusion to Pascal must refer to this line from the *Pensées*: "The last act is bloody, however fine the comedy may be up till then . . ."[12] This suggests an outline or a model for narrative, or perhaps more pertinently, a model for the construction of narrative, a representation of the desire of narratees or readers to reach a tragic end, a death: that is to say, an end that confers meaning on the narrative. *Le Dessous de cartes*, despite the deaths it records, will refuse to furnish so unequivocal an ending. Perhaps the narrator suggests that in the last analysis the desire for and of storytelling – the desire to tell, the desire to listen – subtends all other meanings, in literature as in the psychoanalytic transference. It is this desire that persists when all other wished-for interpretations reveal themselves to be aleatory and undecidable. If nothing else, the reader must recognize his need to take his place at the gaming table, to become a partner in a hand of whist.

We saw that for Benjamin storytelling implicates wisdom, counsel, the sharing and exchange that take place in and by way of live communication. The simulation of orality in writing appears to want to restore this situation of live communication in a medium that is necessarily marked by detachment, solitude, privacy, lack of context. If *Le Dessous de cartes* is typical of a certain effort to recover the oral within the written (typical, to be sure, in a somewhat extreme manner), Barbey's tale seems to tell us that wisdom and counsel no longer can be recovered: if there is a "moral of the story," it can't be formulated; the semantic level of the tale is finally undecidable. But in this labyrinth of the diabolical narrative, there is nonetheless something like a presence: the presence of the narratee to the narrator, the presence of a simulated situation of interlocution which invites, which even demands, the impassioned, even erotic, participation of the reader in the game, his implication in the movement of reference that takes place as the emphasis of the tale slips from narrating to listening. If we may not want to say, with Benjamin, that the reader encounters himself in this type of narrative, the reader must nevertheless come face to face with his inescapable desire for narrative, as the ultimate motivation of oral or written storytelling. It is of course possible that the story will make fun of him. But that is one of the possible vicissitudes of desire that one must accept.

In the tale, such as it appears in the exemplary instance of Barbey, one may detect a commentary on and a critique of the modern novel, the realm of the lonely individual and of the solitary reader. It is not so much that the tale, short story or novella, stands in opposition to the novel – since one could find in many novels an effort on the part of the narrator to establish a dialogue and a transferential relation with the reader – but that by its example it challenges the novel to reclaim something that it has lost from its heritage: the situation of live communication, the presence of voice. These can now only be simulated, fictive, the object of conscious artistic creation, but even as such they may represent an essential aspect of narrative, which is always also narrating, the transmission from a person (if merely grammatical) to another. Those writers who are strongly marked by nostalgia for storytelling – among whom Barbey is a notable example, along with Balzac and Henry James and so many others – look to the past, toward a lost *ancien régime* of narrative, yet at the same time they may be opening the way toward a more "writeable" literature (to use the term which Barthes sets in opposition to "readable"), one where the reader must engage the very medium and communicative situation of narrative, where, if he enters the transferential space, he cannot fail to discover that he is himself in play in the game, and himself at issue.

Psychoanalysis itself revives the situation of oral narrative exchange. Freud's strictures on traditional therapies for hysteria, and on traditional reports of case histories, suggest his Benjaminian valorization of the situation of live interlocution in the construction of a story, its investments of desire, its effects of truth.[13] And, like Barbey, he suggests that the link between teller and listener that produces the story is originally and ultimately an erotic bond, an investment of otherwise inexpressible desires into narrative exchange. But Freud complicates the vectors of Benjamin's transmission of "wisdom." Does wisdom flow from the storyteller to the listener? Or is it the listener – the analyst – who provides "counsel"? The transferential model suggests that there is an irresolvable shuttling between these two positions: that the truth of narrative is situational, the work of truth reciprocal. Wisdom comes from conviction, however you construct it.

NOTES

1 See Roman Jakobson, "Closing Statement: Linguistics and Poetics," in *Style in Language*, ed. T. Sebeok (Cambridge, Mass.: MIT Press, 1960), pp. 350–77.

2 See Guy de Maupassant, "Une ruse," in *Mademoiselle Fifi*. This tale was first brought to my attention by Angela S. Moger: see her "That Obscure Object of Narrative," *Yale French Studies* 63 (1983), pp. 129–38. My use of the terms "narrative," "story," and "narrating" generally corresponds to Gérard Genette's "*récit*," "*histoire*," and "*narration*," in "Discours du récit," *Figures III* (Paris:

Editions du Seuil, 1972); English trans. Jane Lewin, *Narrative Discourse* (Ithaca: Cornell University Press, 1980). On the questions that interest me in this essay, see also Ross Chambers, *Story and Situation* (Minneapolis: University of Minnesota Press, 1985).

3 See Tzvetan Todorov, "Les Hommes-récits," in *Poétique de la prose* (Paris: Editions du Seuil, 1971), pp. 78–91; English trans. Richard Howard, *The Poetics of Prose* (Ithaca: Cornell University Press, 1977).

4 Honoré de Balzac, *Autre étude de femme*, in *La Comédie humaine* (Paris: Bibliothèque de la Pléïade, 1976), 3: 674. Further references to this tale will be given in parentheses in my text.

5 Balzac himself uses the story in another context, in *La Muse du départment*.

6 Walter Benjamin, "Der Erzähler: Betrachtungen zum Werk Nikolai Lesskows," in *Illuminationen* (Frankfurt a. Main: Suhrkamp Verlag, 1955), p. 409; English trans. Harry Zohn, "The Storyteller: Reflections on the Works of Nikolai Leskov," in *Illuminations* (New York: Schocken Books, 1969), p. 83. I shall generally follow the translation by Harry Zohn, introducing a few modifications to emphasize the literal sense of the German text. I shall give in parentheses in my text first the page number of the German original, then the page number of the English translation.

7 See Paul Valéry, "Les Broderies de Marie Monnier," *Oeuvres*, ed. Jean Hytier (Paris: Bibliothèque de la Pléïade, 1960), 2: 1244.

8 On these questions, see the excellent exposition by Walter J. Ong, in *Orality and Literacy: The Technologizing of the Word* (London and New York: Methuen, 1982), especially ch. 4, "Writing Restructures Consciousness."

9 See Roland Barthes, *S/Z* (Paris: Editions du Seuil, 1970), pp. 95–6; English trans. Richard Miller, *S/Z* (New York: Hill and Wang, 1975). On narrative as contract and as gift, see also the fine article by Léo Mazet, "Récit(s) dans le récit: l'échange du récit chez Balzac," *L'Année balzacienne*, 1976 (Paris: Garnier: 1976), pp. 129–61.

10   For Bakhtin, see especially "Discourse in the Novel," in *The Dialogic Imagination*, ed. Michael Holquist (Austin: University of Texas Press, 1981), pp. 259–422; for Lacan, "Intervention sur le transfert," in *Ecrits* (Paris: Editions du Seuil, 1966), pp. 215–26; and *Le Séminaire: Livre VIII: Le transfert* (Paris: Editions du Seuil, 1991).

11   Jules Barbey d'Aurevilly, *Le Dessous de cartes d'une partie de whist*, in *Les Diaboliques*, ed. Jean-Pierre Seguin (Paris: Garnier/Flammarion, 1967), p. 174. Further references will be given in my text. Translations here are my own. There is a fairly recent English translation available: "The Story behind a Game of Whist," in *The She-Devils*, trans. Jean Kimber (London: Oxford University Press, 1964). On the *Diaboliques* and this tale, see especially Jacques Petit, *Essais de lectures des "Diaboliques"* (Paris: Lettres Modernes, 1974) and Jean Verrier, "Le Dessous d'une Diabolique," *Poétique* 9 (1972), pp. 50–60.

12   Pascal, *Pensées*, Edition Chevalier, no. 227.

13   See in particular the famous passage in *Studies on Hysteria* where Freud, in a kind of *ars poetica*, notes that "it still strikes me myself as strange that the case histories I write should read like short stories and that, as one might say, they lack the serious stamp of science" (*SE* 2:60). He goes on to suggest the advantage of such narrative accounts.

Constructing Narrative:
An Interview with Peter Brooks

conducted by John S. Rickard and Harold Schweizer

SCHWEIZER It might be useful to begin by asking you to draw a context for your work in narrative theory. I think of authors like Walter Benjamin, Paul Ricoeur, Frank Kermode, Hillis Miller or, of course, Freud, who might have influenced you.

BROOKS I think actually my work in narrative theory developed originally rather untheoretically, from readings of novels themselves. But I was hit in quite a decisive way, I would say, by structuralist and narratological work coming out of France in the late sixties and early seventies. I suppose the most important practical influence on my work was putting together a course along with some colleagues (primarily Michael Holquist, Adam Parry, and Alvin Kernan), a course originally referred to as "Literature X" – the unknown – which later became Literature 120, "Narrative Forms," the introductory course to the Literature Major at Yale. Our groping towards a course that would talk about narrative as a large literary kind in a – how shall I put it – quasi-anthropological context was very important to my own thinking. In terms of actual critical sources, I would say that probably Roland Barthes, was the key influence, Barthes and to some extent early Tzvetan Todorov, the Todorov of *Poetics of Prose*, and also Gérard Genette. Then I moved back, to the Russian Formalists, whom I found always lucid and illuminating. And then forward from them to read people like Bakhtin and Benjamin and Hillis Miller, whom you mentioned. These have been important but they came in at a somewhat later stage.

SCHWEIZER   What about Frank Kermode?

BROOKS   Well, yes, Frank Kermode. *The Sense of an Ending* was an extraordinarily productive book for me, and a book that is *sui generis*. I mean there really was nothing like it before or after. In its own way, it was a structuralist study of narrative, but posed the question in larger, more philosophical contexts. So that indeed it is a very important book. Through the perspective of Kermode, I began to pay more attention to Sartre's work on narrative, both in *La Nausée* and in *Les Mots*, which still seems to me very brilliant.

SCHWEIZER   Since your theoretical work, as you point out, developed untheoretically, is it fair to say then that you might consider the relationship between theory and literature problematic? We obviously can't just apply a theory to a literary text, can we?

BROOKS   My own belief is that "application" is the wrong model for the use of theoretical models. When you apply theory to texts it implies that you're putting some sort of a grid over them, and this may be quite reductive and limiting. I prefer to think in terms of an interference of two systems, where you start from two different places, one in the literary text, the other in theoretical considerations, and try to see what their merger looks like, and what happens as they start to contaminate one another, as you create a sort of effect of superimposition of one on the other (and vice versa), which is what I try to do particularly in the use of psychoanalysis. I suppose that the most anthologized piece I've ever written is the essay (which became a chapter of *Reading for the Plot*) called "Freud's Masterplot." It's very curious how that came about. It developed really just as a hunch that came from reading certain novels, especially Balzac's, and particularly his *La Peau de chagrin*, which I don't talk much about in *Reading for the Plot*. It's almost too obvious a case of discovery of the death drive under the pleasure principle. But the essay really derived from reading texts like that and saying: This sounds like something in Freud. Would it be illuminating to read *Beyond the Pleasure Principle* as a template for narrative plot? So I went back to the text, the Freud text, and the more I got into it the more I found it extraordinarily suggestive. But the essay was written . . . you see, that was the vector of it, it was moving from literature, from novels, toward trying to find some generalizable grounds for their study, and something that might enable one to talk in a more synthetic way about narrative plot.

RICKARD   Clearly, however, psychoanalysis is more than just another theory for you. In your response to Terence Cave's review of *Reading for the Plot* you assert that despite the "embarrassment" of earlier psychoanalytic criticism, of older Freudian readings, that there is an anthropological importance to psychoanalytic criticism that depends on Freud having understood the structure of the mind, the mental apparatus, correctly. Does Freud really give us a model that reaches beyond intertextuality and metaphoricity? In your discussion of transference and construction, you mention the possibility of a referentiality that does not name the world; in what sense is Freud's work truly referential?

BROOKS   In the first place, I think you have to accept certain basic Freudian hypotheses as true for you. I mean if you are someone who rejects the notion of the unconscious, or of unconscious mental process, then I think psychoanalysis is not going to work for you. But if Freud generally seems to correspond to your notion of how psychic process works, then the interest of the Freudian reference is that you have essentially a kind of stereoptic effect because you have two approaches to the same thing. Or say, rather, one approach which is to mind directly, in Freud – but not all that directly because Freud is always talking about the products of mind, whether it be in dreams, in jokes, in people trying to tell their life stories or whatever – and another approach which is through literature as a product of mind. The point at which these two converge does, I think, throw things into an interesting perspective or relief, and that is what I am interested in. Superimposing these two models of psychic process and its products ought to tell you something about the dynamics of literary texts. I'm not interested in the "dynamics of literary response" as studied by Norman Holland, among others. The terminology I use could lead to some confusion because he also talks about "dynamics," but he's much more interested in what goes on in an individual reader and how a specific text will activate things from that reader's psychic life. I'm much more interested in how the reader's psychic life activates the text. I remain in some ways an unreconstructed formalist, I realize that more and more the older I get, particularly in a world where we're surrounded by cultural studies and what appears at times as a total dissolution of the text.

RICKARD   So if I want to apply your insights from *Reading for the Plot* to my own readings, does it matter whether Freud is true or not? Could I use your insights, thinking of Freud simply as someone who wrote at the same time as so many of these novelists were writing who may have been formed by those same influences, as just another literary system?

BROOKS   You can do that, and it is certainly true that Freud is just another literary product of, say, the late Romantic and modernist era. But it seems to me if you say that, the *truth* that you come out with is a bit different; it is a cultural truth. You say that these two types of texts both can be described in terms of the same cultural evolutions. I would want to go further than that and say that if you're willing to give a certain credence to the Freudian model of psychic process, it can illuminate literature by showing how it is part of psychic process – while literature in turn can illuminate psychic process. Psychoanalysis and literature are mutually illuminating: according to psychoanalysis, man is a fiction-making animal, one defined by fantasies and fictions. Freud, of course, was the first to say that the poets and the philosophers had been there before him.

It's interesting, I was just discussing the Freud essay on narcissism with my class the other day. It's a very complex and in some ways confused essay, and I found myself sorry that I had assigned it. But I was struck by how he chooses here to take on absolutely the most literary of subjects – not only the Ovidian reference: what could be more a literary subject than narcissism in all its forms? Freud just has to take it on and has to bring it into psychoanalytic theory, as a key part of that theory. Which is to say that in one sense what Freud is (you might say, all Freud is) is a reinterpretation of late Romantic culture in terms of the mental configurations produced in essentially cultivated bourgeois Europeans of the late nineteenth and early twentieth century. But that in itself is not negligible.

RICKARD   But you would want to go beyond that in terms of seeing the unconscious or the function of the unconscious as a producer of narrative itself.

BROOKS The unconscious, yes, and also Freud's whole view of human personality and identity. A cornerstone of Freud's work for me is the *Three Essays on the Theory of Sexuality* and his view of the sexual constitution of human beings makes considerable sense to me – using sexuality in the largest sense, what Juliet Mitchell in a recent article calls "psycho-sexuality." Again, it's a conception of the human subject very much present in late Romantic culture, in subdued or submerged forms, but Freud makes it explicitly a description of human character and that to me is also very important.

SCHWEIZER But, one could ask if there are any other sources of desire other than sexuality, couldn't one?

BROOKS You could. I think Freud's concept of sexuality, and of libido, is elastic enough so that, while maintaining that the sexual instincts or drives are always primary, it opens up – by the time he gets into the 1920s – to the concept of eros, as that which binds all living substance together. So it becomes sufficiently broad and elastic, almost too much so. But it is always originally sexual, or let us say, psycho-sexual, because what it is really based on is the notion that human desire comes into being from its very origin predicated on lack, severance and prohibition. As determined by the "law" of "castration," desire is always inhabited by lack, and by its very nature never fulfillable, always driven by unconscious scenarios of impossible fulfillment. And that corresponds, I suppose, to my own personal understanding of human beings. I think Freud is essentially a tragic humanist. That's a major strain in Western thought, and one that I think he renews in very forceful ways.

SCHWEIZER You go to Freud without making much use of Lacan, at least without making much overt use of

Lacan. You seem not to need the kind of revisionary reading of Freud that Lacan performs.

BROOKS   The true Lacanians will denounce me, but I have become convinced that Lacan really is not a systematic thinker but rather a series of brilliant glosses to Freud. Reading his seminar on the transference, which I had to work through to review it last fall, reinforced that conviction. He's brought some new terminology and some refinements of Freudian conceptions, but I think that he is most of all a brilliant reader of Freud who works out of a context that Freud didn't have, in structural linguistics. So, I tend to go back to Freud and use Lacan to illuminate Freud. I may use Lacan more in my new book. What I've found particularly interesting are some of the British psychoanalysts who themselves have been influenced by Lacan, Juliet Mitchell, whom I find very helpful, and Gregorio Kohon, an Argentine, I believe, who works in Britain and writes in English. And of course Jacqueline Rose. I think the Rose-Mitchell collection *Feminine Sexuality* is among the best work done on Lacan, and what we can learn from Lacan. But I do find myself continually going back to Freud himself.

I've never had a sense of – how shall I put it – an agenda laid out in front of me, of where I want to go, nor have I ever had a sense of any very firm theoretical grounding in what I'm doing. It's been very much a matter of *bricolage* as I go along, discovering what seems to make sense. I didn't come to Freud all that early, not at all when I was a student. If you ever went back to *The Novel of Worldliness*, my first book, you would find it totally innocent of Freud. It was only some time in the late sixties that I began reading Freud in a serious way. My education at Harvard was quite traditional.

RICKARD   I'd like to raise again a question you faced last night about the place of non-Western narratives in your thinking. Can we say that Freud gives us a "master-plot" that is true for all narratives, or is there a different mind at work in Japanese or African narratives, for example?

BROOKS I'm just not competent to answer that. The question of whether the Oedipus complex is universal, for instance, is one which has received a lot of attention from anthropologists. Certainly what I was citing from my Chinese student – about the lesser attention given to temporality in Chinese language – seems to me very significant and a major difference from the language and literature of the West. On the other hand, you can say that everyone is born of a mother, at least, so that all infants go through the experience of oneness with the mother's body and severance from it. The relation to the maternal body is absolutely essential, as Melanie Klein – working on several suggestions in Freud – has shown. It's hard to think that there is any human being anywhere who doesn't share some of those symbolic formations which develop from relationship to the maternal body. The nuclear family has been certainly eroded, if not exploded. Nonetheless, to the extent that desire toward and for the maternal body always is going to be prohibited, whether there is a father there to prohibit it or not, it would seem that some form of the castration complex, broadly interpreted, is also almost universal. The fact that incest, so far as we know, is quite universally taboo, as Lévi-Strauss points out, does suggest that there are certain constants of the Freudian family drama that you really can't get away from.

RICKARD Certainly you are interested in the structure of narrative in terms of beginnings, middles and ends, which would be where some people might raise an argument about circular narratives, about other kinds of narratives. Is that sense of beginning, middle and end, that sense of death giving meaning to narrative again something that is specifically born of our culture? Obviously death is a universal experience, but it seems that many different cultures have narrative ways of getting around that.

BROOKS They do, and there certainly are cultures in which death is possibly reabsorbed into life in more creative ways, is attenuated in ways it's not in Western culture. Still, every known culture has to deal with death as a termination and as the other side of life. They do it in different ways but you can't say that in any culture it is insignificant.

SCHWEIZER It could be a male paradigm, though, couldn't it, particularly when the notion of the finality of death makes us think of narratives as having "discharges" and reaching "climaxes" and so forth. Feminists might wish to look for different kinds of narrative paradigms.

BROOKS Certainly that paradigm has been criticized by feminists. A couple of articles, particularly one by a former student of mine, Susan Winnett, in *PMLA*, claimed that the model of arousal, tumescence, discharge is purely phallic and masculine. I'm not sure, physiologically speaking, that it is so purely phallic. It certainly applies to female physiology as well and what Susan Winnett comes up with as a specifically female plot strikes me as a bit debatable. But I am perfectly willing to accept the criticism that I've given essentially a phallic model. One thing I'm trying to consider in the material I'm preparing to present tonight, mainly on George Eliot, is how some women authors working within a masculinist tradition predicated on looking at women's bodies, and so on, manage to subvert it. Later in the same book with the material on Eliot, I have a fairly long section on Marguerite Duras, who is interesting because she very much accepts the whole visual framing of the woman's body – as you know, she has worked as a filmmaker as well as a novelist – but then works very subtle displacements within it, so that the girl with the lover in *L'Amant*, the book I discuss, is always looking at herself being looked at, so that she becomes a kind of reflective surface which is not entered by the gaze. But the model of the presence of death doesn't seem to me either masculinist or feminist. I think it may be Western but it seems to me that it has a fairly universal applicability within Western culture.

SCHWEIZER A question about violence. Jay Clayton quotes Leo Bersani as saying that there exists a complicity between narrativity and violence, a violence that one would find rather quickly in Freud's Dora case or in the Wolf Man chapter in *Reading for the Plot*. In Freud's analysis of the Wolf Man Freud insists on determining a primal scene whose particularity is shocking because it is so totally unsupported by the patient himself. Nevertheless, even in his later revisions of the case, Freud's interpretive drive does not abate, it still drives the Wolf Man, one might say, with the power of a hermeneutical compulsion towards a certain origin and end. You don't seem to want to criticize that hermeneutical violence, that determination of Freud's to find a cause for which he cannot find support.

BROOKS Well, I suppose that may be all of us who are critics or philosophers or interpreters participate in some form of hermeneutical violence. That is, after all, our business. I don't find Freud's hermeneutical violence more totalitarian than others; in fact, against Stanley Fish or against Clayton, I would maintain that Freud, read carefully, is actually full of doubts about his hermeneutical schemata. Reading through Freud, particularly chronologically, is a process of constant revision, constant theoretical readjustment and constant overlay so that, though he can sometimes sound rather dogmatic and he is, after all, trying to establish a new science of the mind and needs to grasp on to certain principles, primal scenes being one of them, it seems to me it's a much less closed and monolithic discourse than many people think.

SCHWEIZER   But should we not proceed with hermeneutical curiosity rather than with hermeneutical violence? Is it not violent to claim origins and causes that cannot be supported by evidence? In Freud's Wolf Man case the primal scene seems totally invented, without any empirical support.

BROOKS   It's true, of course, that it's found because of the effects that it has to explain. It is postulated essentially because Freud wants to find an origin, a cause to explain the effects, and so he reconstitutes it. This really is an example of "construction," such as I was talking about last night. The violence then comes in asserting that the construction is a reality. But, as you know, in those two long footnotes he added to the text of the Wolf Man, he reopens the question and throws doubt upon the reality of the "primal scene," though he does then conclude that he thinks it's more likely that it really happened. He also says it doesn't really matter. In the *Introductory Lectures*, he returns to that question and says, essentially, primal scene, primal fantasy, who cares? So there is a double movement in his thinking. It's a bit like the end of *Totem and Taboo*, where he quotes Goethe quoting St John, where it's a question of whether in the beginning was the word or in the beginning was the deed. Freud wants it to be a deed, but in the process of making it a deed he is certainly open to deconstructive possibilities, and consciously so. He's not artless about this.

SCHWEIZER You claim that such openness is heroic . . .

BROOKS Well, it is rather heroic for a man who's raised as a late nineteenth-century physiologist to open up these possibilities, or to turn to Plato and the myth of the androgyne to explain the origin of sexuality.

RICKARD In your discussion of the transference you make some very suggestive analogies between reader and text and analyst and analysand. But in that particular case we have the interesting situation where the text, as it were, the analysand, was able, as you know, to contest that interpretation. When Karin Obholzer interviewed the Wolf Man, he said that although Freud told him that he would remember, "I've always thought the memory would come but it never did." And Ned Lukacher claims that, "as far as the Wolf Man is concerned, psychoanalysis stands self condemned by virtue of its deduction of causes from effects." The Wolf Man instead maintained that it was his seduction by his sister that lay at the origin of his neurosis. So there you've got a real agon, a real contest where the "text" is fighting back.

BROOKS Those Obholzer interviews, though, are themselves subject to accusations of hermeneutical violence because she so wants to be critical of Freud, to say that Freud got it all wrong and that it really was the sister. By the end you have the feeling that she is harassing him every bit as much as Freud ever did. Poor old Wolf Man. And, of course, he wrote his own memoirs, which treat Freud with elaborate respect, which is why it is hard to take some of Obholzer at face value. He talks of Freud as if he were a god. The Wolf Man's memoirs are so funny and so sad. He has an infected tooth and he keeps going to dentists, and each one turns out to be named Doctor Wolf. Then he has to go back into analysis with Ruth Mack Brunswick, and she is involved in a considerable rivalry with the other Freud disciples, and she tries to destroy his belief that he had a special relation to Freud and a special foundational role in psychoanalysis. So the poor guy becomes both the whipping boy and the guinea pig for the formation of psychoanalytic doctrine, and I think it's absolutely right that he ends up belonging to the Freud archives.

RICKARD To what extent was Freud's own reading of the Wolf Man determined by his own competition with Jung and Adler? At the end of the "Constructions in Analysis" essay you see him looking to Jung and Adler. Perhaps one of the reasons he needs to find that primal scene is to verify his hypothesis of infant trauma and the importance of infant trauma in psychoanalysis. His reading was determined to some extent also by competition.

BROOKS Oh, absolutely, and by the polemic with Jung in particular. And I think his choice of material to write up in many instances is determined by his need to create elbow room for himself in the psychoanalytic movement.

RICKARD You have said that reader response criticism often makes excessive claims for the role of the reader to the point of abolishing the semiotic constraint that the text exercises upon reading. Where does that semiotic constraint come into play with Freud and the Wolf Man, for example? He called himself "the conquistador," and at times Freud's readings do seem procrustean in terms of the needs that Freud has. Are you comfortable with that model in terms of a model for reader response?

BROOKS Well, no, I don't think readers should be conquistadors. Freud certainly thought that he had certain constraints. With the Wolf Man, for instance, the text of the dream as recounted by the Wolf Man is there as a constraint. You may say that he sets very few constraints on his ways of interpreting the dream, yet he does, by that point, have the basic terminology, the basic procedures of the dreamwork – condensation and displacement and figurability and so on. So, I don't think it's a completely lawless or constraint-free interpretation. The "Constructions" essay suggests that he would say the analyst cannot simply recreate the text in his own head because he's got to feed it back to the analysand, and if the analysand shows no sign of recognition, no sign of conviction, then it won't do any harm but it also won't do any good, and it's got to be dropped from the hypothesis.

SCHWEIZER It's kind of hard to understand why it wouldn't do any harm, isn't it?

BROOKS Well, in Freud's terms, non-recognition by the analysand makes that piece of construction simply fall away. It's like an arrow that bounces off the armor, if you will.

SCHWEIZER Isn't that quite idealistic?

RICKARD Doesn't fit the puzzle so it doesn't belong.

BROOKS There is no sign of recognition. Whether that's true or not, I'm not sure, but certainly that's always his argument.

SCHWEIZER If the unconscious is the timeless, the untold or the incomprehensible, if it might constitute a truth that we subject to narration and temporality, are we then not falsifying what we narrate? To say this differently, do not our narratives have an origin so inscrutable that it cannot ever be sufficiently discovered or explained?

And, if that is so, maybe then psychoanalysis is interminable.

BROOKS   Absolutely. I wouldn't disagree with any of that. That's maybe what Conrad's sentence from *Lord Jim* that I used as an epigraph to *Reading for the Plot* is saying. These are utterances which really are interminable. We have to find certain periodicities for them because we are time bound. We cannot submit ourselves to the timelessness of the unconscious. We don't have enough time. In a sense, that's what psychoanalysis does, or tries to do: submit itself to the timelessness of the unconscious, which is one reason why it's never been and never will be a popular undertaking. It's probably a dying undertaking at the moment. People don't have the time and the money for it and real psychoanalysis is becoming more and more confined, I think, to pedagogic psychoanalysis. Other forms of psychotherapy use some of the apparatus of psychoanalysis but they are not analysis in that sense.

SCHWEIZER   So how do we understand Freud's setting a time limit to the Wolf Man's case? That was a particular kind of violation of the nature of psychoanalysis itself, wasn't it?

BROOKS   Well, it's something he did quite often, the idea being that if you set a terminus, then it speeds up the process of overcoming resistances and producing fresh material that's been repressed. But he never thought that what he got as a result was in any sense a complete or final analysis. As "Analysis Terminable and Interminable" says, the dynamics of the transference and the approaching end and resistance to the end can always produce fresh material and can make analysis interminable.

RICKARD   Your reading of *Heart of Darkness* is in some ways a nice metaphor for Freud's career in terms of Marlow and Kurtz and that sense of seeking a full utterance and then finding, not necessarily "the horror, the horror," but a voice that doesn't speak a full utterance, that can never give a full utterance.

BROOKS   That's nice. And you might also think of Lévi-Strauss's narrative in *Tristes Tropiques*, which is trying to get further and further back toward a true savage state, but when you get there it is so savage and so other that you can't communicate with it.

RICKARD   So you're forced into a dialogue rather than a summing up, as you put it.

BROOKS   Or you're forced into a kind of interpretation of the signs, rather than any feeling that you really have grasped its essence.

RICKARD   What about the way memory works in narrative? What's the relationship between memory and desire in narrative? You talk about the tension between eros and thanatos, one force moving forward and one moving back. How does memory fit in? Is it a form of desire itself?

BROOKS   I think memory works both ways, in that the returns that I talk about, for instance in *Great Expectations*, are both returns to and returns of: moments when the past seems to come forward, as in the return of the repressed, or when memory takes us back into the past. So it's a shuttling movement. But the relationship between memory and desire: it occurred to me the other day (this is again thinking through Benjamin) that one of the great forms of modern consciousness – I'm not sure it's nearly so strong before the nineteenth century as it is then and afterwards – is nostalgia. Nostalgia has always existed, you have it in the elegy and and in the Roman poets, certainly. But it seems to me that the nineteenth century really makes nostalgia a major mode of consciousness, and one of the premises of nostalgia – I was thinking of writing a book about nostalgia – is that paradise is always lost, it is always in a temporal relation of irretrievability. Proust says at some point that the true paradises are the paradises that we have lost. The very notion of paradise is bound up with its loss, it's the optics of loss. The first person who puts this persuasively in terms of the individual's life is Rousseau, who first presents the notion that childhood is absolutely formative, that you have to keep in touch with it, yet that it exists also as a kind of mythic Eden that cannot be recovered. So that I suppose that memory . . . the connection of memory and desire in the nineteenth century is partly one of memory of a form of satisfaction which is foreclosed to one, and not completely comprehensible, but nonetheless a feeling that there was once a greater plenitude, unity, whatever. There's a Wordsworthian version of that, obviously.

RICKARD Would that work well as a definition for the modernist sense of plot?

BROOKS I wonder. I think it is certainly one major strain in plot, and particularly in plots of individual *Bildung*, which very often seem to be either undermined by or somehow attached to the past so that no progress forward is entirely satisfactory.

RICKARD Perhaps the simultaneous suspicion of plot and nostalgia for plot in *Heart of Darkness* or *Ulysses* characterizes modernist fiction?

BROOKS Those would be good examples. Proust, again, would be the obvious model. But Faulkner too. I think of Caddie and Quentin.

SCHWEIZER   Can there be a novel that has no nostalgia for plot?

BROOKS   Good question. I'm not sure. Perhaps in some of the early picaresque, where you have a feeling that life is, how shall I put it, a constant flight forward with no regrets. Something like *Lazarillo*. In a way those are pre-nostalgic novels, and also almost pre-individualistic novels, according to our modern sense of individual identity.

RICKARD   In *Reading for the Plot* and even in the beginning of *The Melodramatic Imagination* you construct a history of plot that is a decline from sacred narratives to realist narratives to modernist narratives to what we would call, for lack of a better term, postmodernist narratives. Christopher Lehmann-Haupt, in praising your book, argues that you arrive at something of a dead end at the end of *Reading for the Plot* in terms of where we go next in fiction. I would think from your work that you would be very dissatisfied or distrustful of a truly postmodernist novel and consider it in some ways broken or, in terms of a student's question last night, insane in some way. Is it desirable at all to have insane or broken narratives? Is there a place for "mad art?"

BROOKS   I think so, and I think there is some great mad art: Gérard de Nerval, for instance – real narratives of schizophrenia. The only thing I would quarrel with in your description of my argument is the word "decline." I see a movement out from under sacred history, which in some narrative could be a fall but it's also a liberation. As for postmodernist narratives, broken narratives, there maybe was a form of postmodernist experimentation which became a bit tedious, some of the greater refinements of the new novel in France. I really liked the early new novel experimentation, the early Robbe-Grillet,

Butor, Sarraute, Duras. Some of the later incarnations, such as Philip Sollers' novels, became tedious to me.

But what I think happened after that, particularly with the coming of the Latin American novel (and a certain North American novel) was the return to plot in a parodic way. I talk about that a little at the end of my book. I have in mind writers like Vargas Llosa and Puig. Puig is one of the best examples because he loves movie plots; think of *Betrayed by Rita Hayward*, for example. My sense is that at the present moment, while we have lost our belief in plots, in the replete sense of Dickens' plots, we can't do without plotting. Many postmodern narratives – be it Robbe-Grillet or Pynchon or Puig or whatever – love plotting. It's plotting that often doesn't lead anywhere if by "somewhere" you mean the Dickensian ending, but certainly we still are convinced that there are lines of plot that need to be unravelled. To give up plot completely would be to give up one of our major conceptions of the world as a kind of enigma to be deciphered.

SCHWEIZER Could we bring the lyric into this discussion of plotting and narratives? If narrative moves along a metonymic process in order to obtain metaphoric totality, what does this imply about the lyric, which I associate with metaphoric totality or condensation? To me that would be a different form of desire, but I realize that you talk about the lyric in the same temporal and spatial forms – that is, in terms of postponement and dilatory space – as when you talk about long narratives. Doesn't the lyric represent a different kind of desire than the one we find in narrative, the more since you claim that narratives require some length to work through desire?

BROOKS I think that's right. One ideal of the lyric would be represented by the Imagist poem which condensed statement into the most compact and richest symbolic juxtaposition, as in some famous Ezra Pound two-line poems. That is one ideal to which lyric strives. It can be perfectly true that there is some narrative movement in a lyric. A sonnet, for instance, has a movement and has a kind of typical template of movement. But I think that the difference may be that the argument that a sonnet is making doesn't really depend on temporal succession. It depends much more on a form of address, the way it solicits the response of the listener. I think that's quite different and the form of attention that you pay to a lyric and to a narrative is really quite different. A lyric requires that once you read it to the end, then you read it backward again, and this creates a kind of shuttling movement – the kind of thing that Jakobsen talks about in his formal analysis of the role played by rhyme, for instance, and meter, the way you're always being brought back and made to discover parallelisms, connections that you didn't necessarily detect the first time through. So everything in a lyric is trying to make you grasp it as a total structure, and narrative works differently.

SCHWEIZER   That would suggest the timeless again, wouldn't it? Then one could say that the lyric attempts some sort of avoidance of narrative, an avoidance of the falsifications of narrative as if a narrative was stopping by woods on snowy evenings or on Westminster bridges to look into itself.

BROOKS   Absolutely. Lyrics are very often about moments of arrest and they're thematically so often about the defeat of time, in the mode of the Shakespearian sonnet. Narratives, even Proust, aren't about the defeat of time. They can be about the *recovery* of time, as Proust claims to be. That's rather different.

RICKARD   There seem to be those important lyric moments though, in Proust or in Joyce – Joyce's epiphanies, for example – where you have a breaking open of the narrative or, to put it in your terms, a localized discharge of narrative energy that occurs within a longer prose fiction. Does that partake of a different kind of energy than what you would describe as the metonymy of the middle space? Do these moments still unpack and deploy narrative energy, or is there some sort of releasing of extra energy, a sort of lyric incorporation into narrative?

BROOKS   In a way those are fallings out of time, I would say, a little bit like the Wordsworthian "spots of time" which are both moments of hyper-significance and also moments of silence as well.

RICKARD   Which can then perhaps be reincorporated into a plot, as in *A Portrait of the Artist as a Young Man*, for example.

BROOKS   Of course. Or as in *The Prelude*, where they are reincorporated into the plot.

SCHWEIZER   Freud's insistence on the human being as a storytelling animal – that creature, as James Olney puts it, compelled to tell a story over and over again in the hope of one day getting it to come right – seems to reflect the philosopher's dream for truth. The poet dreams of being remembered rather than understood, doesn't he?

BROOKS   You think so? A poet dreams of being remembered rather than understood? I think the assumption is that the two things will come together, right? And maybe not right away but in some convergence in a future moment when he will be understood because he is remembered and remembered because he is understood. It's a little bit like Stendahl, to talk about a very non-poetic writer, who says, "I take out a lottery ticket, to be read a hundred years from now."

SCHWEIZER Walter Benjamin seems to have seen narratives as communal – social rather than philosophi-cal. Benjamin talks, in this context, of a certain conden-sation or density – *Gedrungenheit* is the word he uses – of stories which he claims makes a story unavailable to psychoanalysis, and the more it is unavailable to psycho-analysis, the more, he says, it can be remembered and retold.

BROOKS But if I'm not mistaken, he's talking specific-ally about the tale at that point, the oral tale which participates in the life of the community and is a kind of transmission of wisdom from one man to another man. It is very much a part of human communication. He has that lovely image of the storyteller's personality clinging to the story like a potter's fingers to the clay pot. But then he goes on to say that the reader of a novel is lonelier than any other reader because it is a form for solitude, which I think is absolutely right. He's referring to Lukács in *The Theory of the Novel*. So, I think the novel is, in a way, an artificial invention of community, it's a fictive community because the novel is both written and read in solitude. The novel is typically something you read alone, at home, when you've bought the book or rented it from the lending library – it's an anti-communal experience.

RICKARD You claimed last night that power has become a central idol perhaps too much worshipped in literary criticism. So much recent theory focuses itself on the political and the ideological, on the ways that desire and narrative are determined by social and economic forces outside the individual. From that point of view, desire and narrative are the results or even the servants of external forces, whereas your notion of desire or the psychoanalytic notion of desire seems much more essential and individual – that we're all born with the same basic desires, that we undergo the same basic traumas, that these all arise within the individual and his or her story or history. So how would you contexualize or perhaps defend your work against this assault of the new historicism, Foucault, and so many other theories that insist on extending themselves out into the world?

BROOKS   I admire Foucault very much. I just think that there is a kind of degraded American version of Foucault which wants to identify discourse with power and leave it at that. It doesn't do anything with it. The theory it develops often offers no way to *read* the texts it discusses. It leads rather to dismissing texts, to seeing in Zola's *Nana*, for instance, only a male cultural stereotype of the prostitute's body, and so on. *Nana* is that, of course, but it's also a lot more than that. One of the wonderful things about Zola is that he creates in *Nana* something that's much more charged with energy, and even fear for its own creator, than he at first realizes. *Nana* is out of control, and I don't think we would bother to read the book if it didn't have that kind of dynamism about it. So my main objection to the theoreticians of power à la Foucault is that they too often dismiss rather than read. Whereas I think we always need to learn to read with enhanced intellectual sympathy.

Much of this work carries the implication, which you also find in Foucault, that we know better than the poor old blinded nineteenth century, and we're in a position to denounce its errors and its prejudices. I'm not sure we are. We're only substituting one set of blinders for another. I think some of this work constitutes an arrogant and unhelpful kind of approach to the study of culture.

RICKARD Along the same lines, in her review of *Reading for the Plot* Marianne Hirsch argues that your reading of "All Kinds of Fur," the old folk tale, validates the story's continuing subordination and confinement of women. Her main point is that your approach fails to reveal the ideological implications of formal structures that we tend to take for granted. Are we justified in seeing a narrative desire for beginnings, middles, and ends as natural, essential, and instinctive? How would you defend yourself against the sense that many of these forms themselves need to be decoded or in some way inspected for what they do to us in social life?

BROOKS I'm perfectly willing to concede that she's right, that when I wrote *Reading for the Plot* I was not particularly sensitive to that issue and that that was not my prime consideration. You can say about "All Kinds of Fur" – and you probably should – that it assigns woman to a certain role of coquettry and doesn't allow her to express desire directly; she has to go through a kind of striptease to make herself an object of desire. But that should not be all you say about it, because obviously it is encoding in its narrative very persistent Western cultural attitudes towards the role of woman. I am disturbed by those who seem to believe that the whole purpose of criticism is denouncing ideological deviance and setting the record straight.

SCHWEIZER Nevertheless, we thought that it's interesting that you didn't add any note to the preface in *Reading for the Plot* now that it has come out again, a preface that would explain that the book has certain blindnesses, say, towards feminist issues.

BROOKS I thought of that and I talked a bit about it with Lindsay Waters at Harvard University Press. One could have written an interesting essay on feminist reactions to the book. Maybe I should have, maybe it was just laziness that kept me from it. But it also was a feeling that when you've done a piece of work, there it is and you've got to move on . . .

RICKARD   Which brings us neatly to your most recent work. Both of us admire your essay on "The Body in the Field of Vision." This work on narrative and the body seems to reflect a shift toward the work of feminist theorists of film, the Lacanian notion of the gaze, of Foucault's interest in panopticism or surveillance. Would you care to discuss this new work and its sources and perhaps any rethinking of your earlier ideas about Freud or desire that it has occasioned?

BROOKS   Once again, this started really with literary texts. In fact the original kernel of it had to do with Zola, and thinking about Zola in the context of some of the bad art of his time, particularly representations of the nude in artists like Cabanel and Bouguereau, which I had begun to encounter in museums. Critics had started to talk once again about this salon art. My work moved on from there, and somewhere along the way of thinking about the place of the body in narrative I encountered the work of people like Laura Mulvey and Jacqueline Rose, which I found extraordinarily exciting and productive. It put some of what I had read in Lacan in a new perspective, and gave me a way to think about some of the problems that interested me, without my ever having become fully conversant with all the labyrinthine ways of film theory. If you take the famous Mulvey article on "Visual Pleasure and Narrative Cinema" as your starting point, by the time you reach 1992, the bibliography on that subject is just enormous, and I don't find all of it very convincing. I find some of it applicable only to the cinema and some of it excessively reductive, in its arguments for a rigid gendering of spectatorship. A good recent book by my former colleague, David Rodowick, *The Difficulty of Difference*, attempts to subtle-ize the notion of sexual difference, which has become sort of hypostasized in much film study. But I did find the work in film theory remarkably productive as a way to think about issues of the body.

Now why did I get interested in the body in the first place? There must have been obscure cultural influences working there: when I started this work I thought it was original, but in a few years I realized that everyone else was writing a book about the body, to the point that I am almost embarrassed. But there it is.

RICKARD When we look at the narrative of your work, you seem to be moving towards problematizing even further the crisis of narrative that you reveal in *Reading for the Plot* by emphasizing again the impossibility of full disclosure, the inevitable frustration of epistemophilia. Perhaps you could comment on this notion of epistemophilia and the new ways you're using that term.

BROOKS Yes, I should cite my sources and say that the person who put me on to that term was Toril Moi, in the work that she's doing on Simone de Beauvoir. It's a term that James Strachey uses or coins to translate *Wisstrieb* in Freud. I found it extraordinarily suggestive as a concept because it combines my interest in desire with the cognitive aspect of narrative. I'm concerned with narratives that are built on the desire to know, and where bodies are concerned, so often in the scenarios I'm looking at desire becomes focused on a body which seems to hold in itself the answer to all the enigmas. Not only the object of desire but the object of knowing as well. And when you go back to Freud, particularly the essay on Leonardo da Vinci, that's all there: the desire to see, the desire to possess, the desire to know are all very closely linked together. So that is really what this book is about: epistemophilic narratives of the body.

RICKARD   Barthes, in *Sade/Fourier/Loyola*, proposes the stage as an alternative way of seeing the body. He calls it "the lit body." In that sense of seeing the body in drama I would think you'd find a very different kind of paradigm for staging scopophilia or epistemophilia in terms of the body than you would in the novel.

BROOKS   Drama is tough to deal with because obviously there the constructedness of the body is entirely different – because you've actually got it in front of you. But the only form I know of that can arrest bodies so that they're fixed by the glance is still photography. Because even theater and even cinema, like prose description, have a certain restlessness. Things are always slipping out from under the fixity of your gaze.

SCHWEIZER   Is there a question that we haven't asked that we should have asked?

BROOKS   In terms of future work, I'm really becoming more and more tempted by the weird idea of trying a kind of "man and works" book on Balzac. For a number of years, I've been thinking about the temptation of doing a biography. It's partly, I've got to confess, because biography is one of the few forms that a literary critic can use, in our culture, to reach a large audience. Not that I think Balzac will, but biography has a popularity that literary criticism doesn't have. So I thought for a long time about whether there was anyone's biography I could write. I also realize I'm probably too lazy to sit in someone's attic reading a lot of old letters and ledgers. I've a certain tolerance for archival work, I like some of it, but I don't know if I could do it for several years.

SCHWEIZER You don't have Ronald Hayman's energies . . .

BROOKS That's right. He turns out one a year! I don't know how he does it. Then the idea of trying to reconceive the "man and works" genre appealed to me. So I might do that. I'm also tempted to do a book on character, a concept neglected in most recent narratological work, which I'm currently teaching a course on: character, personality, identity. And you can see in a way how that comes out of the work on the body because attention to the body implicates the question of identity. How do you know that this is *the body*? So, the next step might be a book on character, which would mean trying to look at the range of meaning of that term in English, going on the one hand from a formal narratological definition of an actor in a narrative, an *actant* in Greimas' sense to, on the other hand, a concept in ethics, which has a certain period connotation. Certainly for the Victorians, character becomes everything. I may do that eventually but I realize I've got to do a lot more reading in moral philosophy in which there's been much interesting recent work. I just finished reading Charles Taylor's *Sources of the Self*, a marvelous book for talking about questions like this. So that's one possibility. And I keep thinking of others. I also teach a course with a colleague in the law school on law and literature, particularly on narrative. It tries to address, not only how stories are told at the law, but how they are listened to, and how they become accepted and become operative. Rape cases, for instance, offer competing narratives of the same story elements. The question of confession, when and under what circumstances it's allowable, is another example where narrative is crucial: in *Miranda vs Arizona* and all the cases that preceded it, then that followed and modified it. Law provides rich possibilities for thinking about the uses and implications of narrative, its social enactments.

Peter Brooks:
A Bibliography, 1963–1993

compiled by Mary E. Schoonover

1963

1 "In the Laboratory of the Novel," *Daedalus* 92, no. 2, pp. 265–80.

1968

2 (Preface), *Cassandra*, by John Hawkes (French translation of *Second Skin*) (Paris: Denoël).

1969

3 *The Novel of Worldliness: Crébillon, Marivaux, Laclos, Stendhal* (Princeton: Princeton University Press), 295 pp.
4 (Ed.), *Yale French Studies*, no. 43; reprinted as *The Child's Part* (Boston: Beacon Press, 1972), 169 pp.
5 "Melodrama and Metaphor," *Hudson Review* 22, no. 2, pp. 213–28.
6 "Nouvelle Critique et Critique Nouvelle aux Etats-Unis," *Nouvelle Revue Française*, no. 201 (September), pp. 416–26.
7 "The Fourth World: Paris," *Partisan Review* 36, no. 1, pp. 11–35.

8   "The Rest Is Silence: Hamlet as Decadent," in *Jules Laforgue: Essays in a Poet's Life and Work*, ed. Warren Ramsay (Carbondale, Ill.: Southern Illinois University Press), pp. 93–110.

9   "Toward Supreme Fictions," *Yale French Studies*, no. 43, pp. 5–14.

1971

10   (Ed.), *Western Literature: Volume 3: The Modern World* (New York: Harcourt Brace Jovanovich).

11   "La Critique des pédagogues," in *L'Enseignment de la littérature*, eds Serge Doubrovsky and Tzvetan Todorov (Paris: Plon), pp. 551–64.

1972

12   "Romania and the Widening Gyre," *PMLA* 87, no. 1, pp. 7–11.

13   "The Melodramatic Imagination: The Example of Balzac and James," *Partisan Review* 39, no. 2, pp. 195–212; reprinted in *Romanticism: Vistas, Instances, Continuities*, eds David Thorburn and Geoffrey Hartman (Ithaca: Cornell University Press, 1973), pp. 198–220.

1973

14   (Ed.), *Man and His Fictions* in collaboration with Alvin B. Kernan and J. Michael Holquist (New York: Harcourt Brace Jovanovich).

15   "Man and His Fictions: One Approach to the Teaching of Literature," *College English* 35, no. 1, pp. 40–9.

16   "Virtue and Terror: *The Monk*," *ELH* 40, no. 2, pp. 249–63.

1974

17   "Romantic Antipastoral and Urban Allegories," *Yale Review* 64, no. 1, pp. 11–26.

18 "Symbolization and Fictionmaking," in *Explorations in Psychohistory*, ed. Robert J. Lifton (New York: Simon and Schuster), pp. 214–30.
19 "The Text of Muteness," *New Literary History* 5, no. 3, pp. 549–64.
20 "Une esthétique de l'étonnement," *Poétique* 5, no. 19, pp. 340–56.
21 "Virtue-Tripping: Notes on *Le Lys dans la Vallée*," *Yale French Studies*, no. 50, pp. 150–62.

1976

22 *The Melodramatic Imagination: Balzac, Henry James, Melodrama, and the Mode of Excess* (New Haven and London: Yale University Press; reprinted New York: Columbia University Press, 1985), 235 pp.
23 "Competent Readers," *Diacritics* 6, no. 1, pp. 23–6.
24 "The Aesthetics of Astonishment," *Georgia Review* 30, no. 3, pp. 615–39.
25 "Toward a Critical Reading of Reality," in *Schoolworlds 76*, ed. Donald N. Bigelow (Berkeley: McCutchan), pp. 49–61.

1977

26 "Freud's Masterplot: Questions of Narrative," *Yale French Studies*, no. 55–6, pp. 280–300; reprinted in *Literature and Psychoanalysis*, ed. Shoshana Felman (Baltimore: Johns Hopkins University Press, 1982), pp. 280–300; reprinted in *Contemporary Literary Criticism*, eds Robert Con Davis and Ronald Schleifer (New York: Longman, 1989), pp. 287–99.

1978

27 "Godlike Science/Unhallowed Arts: Language and Monstrosity in *Frankenstein*," *New Literary History* 9, no. 3, pp. 591–605.

28 "L'Invention de l'écriture (et du langage)," *Stendhal Club*, no. 78 (janvier), pp. 183–90.

29 "The Text of the City," *Oppositions*, pp. 7–11.

30 "A Man Named Sue," *New York Times Book Review* 83 (July 30), p. 3.

1979

31 (Ed.), *Genet: A Collection of Critical Essays* in collaboration with Joseph Halpern (Englewood Cliffs, N.J.: Prentice-Hall).

32 "Death of/as Metaphor," *Partisan Review* 46, no. 3, pp. 438–44.

33 "Fictions of the Wolfman: Freud and Narrative Understanding," *Diacritics* 9, no. 1, pp. 72–81.

1980

34 "French Structuralist Theories," in colloboration with Denis Donoghue and Edith Kurzweil, *Partisan Review* 47, no. 3, pp. 397–425.

35 "Repetition, Repression, and Return: *Great Expectations* and the Study of Plot," *New Literary History* 11, no. 3, pp. 503–26.

36 "The Mark of the Beast: Prostitution, Melodrama, and Narrative," *New York Literary Forum* 7, pp. 125–140.

37 "Un Rapport illisible: *Coeur des ténèbres*," *Poétique* 11, no. 44, pp. 472–89.

38 "A Note on Angel Medina's Commentary," *New Literary History* 11, no. 3, pp. 581–2.

39 Review of *Freud, Biologist of the Mind: Beyond the Psychoanalytic Legend* by Frank J. Sulloway, *New York Times Book Review* 85 (February 10), p. 9.

40 Review of *Louis-Ferdinand Celine* by Merlin Thomas, *New York Times Book Review* 85 (May 11), p. 11.

41 Review of *The Letters of Gustave Flaubert, 1830–1857*, ed. Francis Steegmuller, *Nation* 230, no. 12 (March 29), p. 375.

42   Review of *Theatre and Revolution: The Culture of the French Stage* by Frederick Brown, *New York Times Book Review* 85 (September 28), p. 12.

1981

43   "Paris by Night: The Cité, the Prostitute, the Novel," *Skyline* (October), pp. 30–1.

1982

44   "Incredulous Narration: *Absalom, Absalom!*" *Comparative Literature* 34, no. 3, pp. 247–69.

45   "Narrative Transaction and Transference (Unburying *Le Colonel Chabert*)," *Novel* 15, no. 2, pp. 101–10.

46   "The Novel and the Guillotine; or, Fathers and Sons in *Le Rouge et le Noir*," *PMLA* 97, no. 3, pp. 348–62.

47   Review of *Camus* by Patrick McCarthy, *New York Times Book Review* 87 (September 12), p. 1.

1983

48   (Foreword), "Fictionality and Reference," *Poetics Today* 4, no. 1, pp. 73–5.

49   "Intellectuals and Politics," *Partisan Review* 50, no. 4, pp. 594–8.

50   Review of *The Random House Book of 20th Century French Poetry*, ed. Paul Auster, *New York Times Book Review* 88 (January 23), p. 9.

1984

51   *Reading for the Plot: Design and Intention in Narrative* (New York: Alfred A. Knopf, Inc.; reprinted New York: Vintage Books, 1985; reprinted Cambridge, Mass.: Harvard University Press, 1992; Italian trans. Torino: Einaudi, 1993), 363 pp.

52   (Ed., with introduction and notes), *The Wings of the Dove* by Henry James (Oxford: Oxford University Press).

53   "Machines et moteurs du récit," *Romantisme* 14, no. 46, pp. 97–104.

54   "Narrative Desire," *Style* 18, no. 3, pp. 312–27.

1985

55   (Ed.), *Yale French Studies*, no. 69, in collaboration with Shoshana Felman and J. Hillis Miller (Special Issue: *The Lesson of Paul de Man*); reprinted as *The Lesson of Paul de Man* (New Haven: Yale University Press, 1986), 333 pp.

56   "Constructions psychoanalytiques et narratives," *Poétique* 16, no. 61, pp. 63–74.

57   Review of *Flaubert's Parrot* by Julian Barnes, *New York Times Book Review* 90 (March 10), p. 7.

1986

58   "Psychoanalytic Constructions and Narrative Meaning," *Paragraph* 7, pp. 55–76.

59   Review of *Balzac and His Reader: A Study of the Creation of Meaning in "La Comedie Humaine"* by Mary Susan McCarthy, *Revue d'Histoire littéraire de la France* 86, no. 4, pp. 765–8.

60   Review of *France, Fin de Siècle* by Eugen Weber, *New York Times Book Review* 91 (September 14), pp. 15–16.

61   Review of *The Order of Mimesis: Balzac, Stendhal, Nerval, Flaubert* by Christopher Prendergast, *Times Literary Supplement*, no. 4345 (July 11), p. 769.

62   Review of *The Responsibility of Forms: Critical Essays on Music, Art, and Representation* and *The Rustle of Language* by Roland Barthes, *New Republic* 195, no. 21, pp. 45–8.

63   Letter concerning *The Wolf Man* by Sigmund Freud, *Times Literary Supplement*, no. 4360 (October 24), p. 1191.

1987

64   "Excerpts from the Symposium on *The Humanities and the Public Interest:* Whitney Humanities Center, April 5, 1986," in collaboration with Jonathan Culler, A. Barlett Giamatti, and Norman Podhoretz, *Yale Journal of Criticism* 1, no. 1, pp. 183–91.

65   "The Idea of a Psychoanalytic Literary Criticism," *Critical Inquiry* 13, no. 2, pp. 334–48; reprinted in *The Trials of Psychoanalysis,* ed. Françoise Meltzer (Chicago: University of Chicago Press, 1988), pp. 145–60; different version in *Discourse in Psychoanalysis and Literature,* ed. Shlomith Rimmon-Kenan (London and New York: Methuen, 1987), pp. 1–18.

66   "The Melodramatic Body," *Journal: A Contemporary Art Magazine* (Spring), pp. 59–65.

67   "The Storyteller," *Yale Journal of Criticism* 1, no. 1, pp. 21–38.

68   "The Turn of The American," in *New Essays on The American,* ed. Martha Banta (Cambridge: Cambridge University Press), pp. 43–67.

69   Review of *College: The Undergraduate Experience in America* by Ernest L. Boyer, *New York Times Book Review* 92 (March 8), pp. 26–7.

70   Review of *Thresholds* by Gérard Genette, *Times Literary Supplement,* no. 4421 (December 25–31), p. 1436.

1988

71   "Il corpo melodrammatico," in *Forme del melodrammatico,* ed. Bruno Gallo (Milan: Guerini), pp. 177–95.

72   "Intervista a Peter Brooks," *L'Indice* (maggio), pp. 20–1.

73   "Le Conteur. Réflexions à partir de Walter Benjamin," in *Maupassant miroir de la nouvelle,* eds Jacques Lecarme and Bruno Vercier (Paris: Presses Universitaires de Vincennes), pp. 225–42.

74   "Positions: Selections from the Symposium on *Literary Theory and the Curriculum,* Whitney Humanities Center, May 2, 1987," *Yale Journal of Criticism* 1, no. 2, pp. 161–224.

75 "Pour une poétique psychanalytique," *Littérature* no. 71 (octobre), pp. 24–39.

76 "The Tale versus the Novel," *Novel* 21, nos 2–3, pp. 285–91.

77 Review of *The Freud Scenario* by Jean-Paul Sartre, *New Republic* 198, no. 5, pp. 40–2.

78 Review of *The Statue Within* by François Jacob, *New York Times Book Review* 93 (March 27), p. 31.

1989

79 (Ed.), *A New History of French Literature* under the general editorship of Denis Hollier (Cambridge, Mass.: Harvard University Press).

80 "Intrång i det privata. Romanen och den semiotiserads kroppen," *Tidskrift för Litteraturventenskåp*, nos. 2–3, pp. 66–81.

81 "L'Ouverture de l'abîme," *Po & sie*, no. 49, pp. 121–8.

82 "Le corps-récit, ou Nana enfin dévoilée," *Romantisme* 18, no. 63, pp. 66–86.

83 "Psykoanalyse og historieforteljing," *Norsk Litteraer Årbok*, pp. 134–54.

84 "Storied Bodies, or Nana at Last Unveil'd," *Critical Inquiry* 16, no. 1, pp. 1–32.

85 "The Opening of the Depths," in *The French Revolution: Two Hundred Years of Rethinking*, ed. Sandy Petrey (Lubbock: Texas Tech University Press), pp. 113–22.

86 Review of *Reading Poe, Reading Freud: The Romantic Imagination in Crisis* by Clive Bloom and *Psychoanalysis and Fiction* by Daniel Gunn, *Times Literary Supplement*, no. 4476 (January 13–19), p. 40.

1990

87 "Bouillabaisse," *Yale Law Journal* 99, no. 5, pp. 1147–57.

88 "Gauguin's Tahitian Body," *Yale Journal of Criticism* 3, no. 2, pp. 51–90; different version in *The Expanding Discourse: Feminism and Art History*, eds Norma Broude and

Mary D. Garrard (New York: Harper Collins), pp. 331–46.

89   (Translation and introduction), *The Last Judgment of Kings* by Sylvain Maréchal, *Yale Review* 78, no. 4, pp. 583–603.

90   "The Tale versus the Novel," in *Why the Novel Matters: A Postmodern Perplex*, eds Mark Spilka and Caroline McCracken-Flesher (Bloomington: Indiana University Press), pp. 303–10.

91   Review of *French Passions and Intellectuals: 20th Century Manifestos and Petitions* by Jean-Francois Sirnelli and *Birth of Intellectuals, 1880–1900* by Christophe Charle, *Times Literary Supplement*, no. 4566 (October 5–11), pp. 1075–6.

92   Review of *Proust, A Biography* by Ronald Hayman, *New York Times Book Review* 95 (December 23), p. 8.

1991

93   "Out of the Blue: Perilous Authority?" *Yale Alumni Magazine* (Summer), pp. 24–5.

94   "Response to Charles Bernheimer ("Storied Bodies, or Nana at Last Unveiled')," *Critical Inquiry* 17, no. 4, pp. 875–7.

95   "The Body in the Field of Vision," *Paragraph* 14, pp. 46–67.

96   "The Revolutionary Body," in *Fictions of the French Revolution*, ed. Bernadette Fort (Evanston: Northwestern University Press), pp. 35–53.

97   Review of *Tenured Radicals: How Politics Has Corrupted Our Higher Education* by Roger Kimball and *Giants and Dwarfs: Essays, 1960–1990* by Allan Bloom, *Times Literary Supplement*, no. 4582 (January 25), pp. 5–6.

98   "The Proffered Word," Review of *The Purloined Punch-Line: Freud Comic Theory and the Postmodern Text* by Jerry Aline Flieger, *Freud and Fiction* by Sarah Kofman, *Lacan* by Malcolm Bowie, and *Le Séminaire* by Jaques Lacan, *Times Literary Supplement*, no. 4623 (November 8), pp. 11–12.

1992

99 (Introduction), "Constructing Traditions: Renovation and Continuity in the Humanities," *Yale Journal of Criticism* 5, no. 2, pp. 83–90.

100 "How to Make Use of the Culture Wars," *Chronicle of Higher Education* 39, no. 16 (December 9), pp. B 1–2.

101 "Review of *Ariadne's Thread: Story Lines* and *Illustrations* by J. Hillis Miller, *Times Literary Supplement*, no. 4675 (November 6), p. 25.

1993

102 *Body Work: Objects of Desire in Modern Narrative* (Cambridge, Mass.: Harvard University Press), 325 pp.

103 (Ed.), *De la Littérature française* in collaboration with Denis Hollier and Howard R. Bloch (Paris: Bordas).

Index